CREATING AN IMAGINATIVE LIFE

Michael Jones

Order this book online at www.trafford.com
or email orders@trafford.com

Most Trafford titles are also available at major online book retailers.

Print information available on the last page.

ISBN: 978-1-4120-9489-4 (sc)
ISBN: 978-1-4669-3412-2 (e)

Cover Art: Sandy Mcmullen, www.sandymcmullen.com
Cover Design: Nancy Nevala, Hinterland Design,www.hinterland.ca
Interior drawings by artist Fredrick Hagan from his Canadian Shield and Georgian Bay collection.

*Owing to limitations of space, all acknowledgements of permission to reprint previously
published materials can be found on page vi, which is an extension of this copyright page.*

1. Creative ability 2. self actualization (Psychology) 3. Creation (literary, artistic, etc)
4.Jones, Michael, pianist

Trafford rev. 05/12/2020

 www.trafford.com

North America & international
toll-free: 1 888 232 4444 (USA & Canada)
fax: 812 355 4082

There is a story living in us
    that speaks of our place
        in the world.

It is a story that invites us to
love what we love
    and simply be ourselves.
The story is not given to us,
it flows naturally from within;
    to hear it we have only to be silent
for a moment
        and turn our face to the wind.

Michael Jones

For Judy

Acknowledgments

Writing, like piano playing, is a solitary activity, yet I rarely feel that I create alone. These words and thoughts carry within them the inspiration of many people. Although there is not nearly enough space to acknowledge them all, I would like to mention a few:

John Morey and Diane Almond, who first suggested the idea of writing this book; Andrea Malinkovitch, who brought me back to the stories while editing many of the early versions of the manuscript; Jean Donelson, who offered the light of clarity when my writing went too far off track; Mary Jane Ryan, whose final editing suggestions made the book much better than I could have on my own; Dawna Markova, who guided the book to a welcoming home; James Fadiman, who reacquainted me with my storytelling voice; Gary Diggins, for pointing out that I don't cage the animalsI dance with them; Toby Simon, who introduced me to the writings of John Gardner and first asked how I would describe my "musical intelligence"; David Whyte, who reminded me that I had a poetic voice within my own soul; and William Isaacs, who invited me to join the Dialogue Project at the Organization Learning Center at M.I.T. where I could share this voice with others and bring along my piano as well.

I also want to thank all of those who offered insight and encouragement as the manuscript progressed: Kelly Anderson, Anne Aufderheide, Judy Brown, Andy Bryner, Jerry Cellilo, Rita Cleary, Diane Cory, Linda Crawford, Lynn Dhority, Karyn DiCastri, Gary Dover, Sheryl Erickson, Betty Sue Flowers, Sandra Friedman, Ted Fullerton, Connie Gage, Barb Gale, Ben Garber, Christine Harris,

Sue Miller Hurst, Kathy Lanser, Eric Lindert, Connie McDermott, Robert Miley, Lucky Paul, Irene Perikhal, Florence Riley, Suzanne Robinson, Stephanie Ryan, and Wesley Van Linda.

I would also like to thank Carol Wright and Marilyn McGuire for editing and publishing an early version of "The Quinte Hotel" in the *NAPRA Journal,* and Peter Hawes and Bonnie Insull for editing and reprinting a version of "Dancing with the Animals" in *Connections,* published by the Music for People Foundation.

Most important, I offer my heartfelt appreciation to my wife, Judy, whose moon has been a constant reflection of my own sun, and to my parents, Allen and Laura, who encouraged each of us to live original and imaginative lives.

Contents

Our artfulness is not a luxury, but an integral part of ourselves. It is a vitality, an impulse, a place of inner nourishment; it serves as a reminder that, no matter what life brings us, we can always come back to the well.

We're equipped by life, for life; and that life is there to meet us each time we step into the new. When we become too enmeshed or established in the old, life's mystery can no longer reach us: Our eyes grow dull; they can no longer enjoy the magic in the world.

Casey wasn't here for my convenience any more than the rain or the trees or the wind. Instead, he was here to remind me that there was another place from which my knowing could come. He was also the enchanter who was opening my heart to love.

There is a wild part of our nature that refuses to be tamed. Our creations flow from this, but they cannot be called up on demand. It is only through practicing as though they were present that we create a welcoming home within us to which they might come.

Meeting the Dragon

The instinctive and creative part of our nature, the one that waits patiently for the world to be a place of love, seems destined to meet many bullies on the corner, including that part of ourselves that would rather be ruled by fear than let this love be seen.

Music of the Spheres

Although our gifts often act mysteriously, they set us on our road early. They do so by using dreams and experiences to attract our attention and map our way. We are touched; time stands still. For a moment, we sense there is something greater than the concerns that fill our days.

Visitors by the Fire

In this world of wind, water, rock, and pine, I feel like a guest in a place where everything is alive. It asks for my appreciation more than my understanding. There is a part of us that has never been separate from nature; the creativity that lives here lives in us as well.

The Quinte Hotel

My work was not to elevate myself above the workings of the world, but to become intimately engaged with it. And there was more "life" to be found in one night of playing the piano in the Quinte Hotel than in anything else I might do.

Wings on the Wind

We build our careers based upon skills and abilities that may not be our primary strengths. Meanwhile, we forget that we are already masters of something that only we can do. That gift comes to us so naturally that often we don't know we are doing it at all.

One Voice to Sing

Ideally, the forms and structures we create should support rather than impede the creative flow. Our discoveries come from searching for the new and also from unlearning what has gone before. In that moment of emptiness, the mind is open to a new possibility.

Everywhere We Are Is Called Home

We can trust that no matter in what form our actions flow, if they are warmed by the wishes of our heart, then even if our creations lead us into living a gypsy life, whatever we create along the road will hold.

Finding a Musical Intelligence

It is easy to feel profoundly vulnerable and self-conscious when we begin penetrating into the deeper levels of who we are, even when we know that those qualities being released from within us may prove to be our greatest strengths.

Living What We Love

Too often, we end up pushing against the very forces that are the true source of our inspiration and strength. We struggle as if life were a dress rehearsal, rather than rest in the moment-to-moment pleasure of simply being ourselves.

Joining the Dance of Creation

We can each be a part of the emerging chorus, whose collective voice may reawaken the sense of longing and wonder that slumbers still and, in so doing, dissolve some of the layers of doubt and fear that separate us from the fertile ground from which all life comes.

All good things . . . come by grace and grace comes by art and art does not come easy.

Norman Maclean
A River Runs Through It

Following the Songlines of the Heart

Several years ago, I spent some time at an educational center on a remote part of the California coast. I was leaving soon for Japan to give several concerts, so occasionally I used the old upright piano in the corner of the busy dining room to practice after dinner. Behind me there was the steady hum of animated conversation.

Most people were familiar with me and my piano recordings. But there was also a regular turnover of attendees. The young man who joined me on the bench one evening was one of these.

"I enjoy your music," he said when I had finished playing.

I thanked him. I was about to get up from the bench when he added quickly, "There's just one thing . . ."

"What's that?" I asked.

"You sound too much like Michael Jones." Then after pausing for a moment, he added, "You really should develop your own style."

I hesitated for a moment, unsure of what to say.

"I *am* Michael Jones," I said finally, wondering what reaction this might provoke.

He thought about this for the longest time. Then he said, "No you're not!" The certainty in his voice left little room for debate.

For the next few moments we sat on the bench, arguing about who I was; an argument that I was sure I was about to lose.

"Here," I said finally, pulling out my wallet with the driver's license from my hip pocket and pushing it into his hand.

He examined the picture carefully and then looked back at me.

"You *really* are Michael Jones," he said with a whisper. Quickly he apologized, shook my hand vigorously, and rushed off to tell his friends.

I took this opportunity to step outside and listen to the surf breaking up on the rocks below, recalling a similar encounter at a conference a few months before.

"Do you know who you *are?*" someone had said to me there. He was halfway through a bite of vegetarian lasagna when our conversation turned to music and to one of my recordings that he knew well.

It was an important question, because there was a time in my life when I didn't know who I was. I didn't know how my subtle trust in the instinctive and imaginative world fit within the context of the rational and orderly world I inhabited each day. How was I to speak of this realm to others, who were convinced that it either did not exist or, if it did, was simply a world of fantasy that was trivial and irrelevant?

I remembered, as a child, when I wrote my first song. Unsure of its outcome, I worked on it secretly for several days. Once it was done, I was amazed with the sound. It had a melody, a rhythm, a key signature; it had a beginning and an end, and I loved it so much that I played it every day. And yet, while this accomplishment filled my life to the brim, the hours of concentrated effort that I brought to the task seemed irrelevant when seen in the context of the more urgent demands that were then being asked of me. There was homework to do and errands to run. I was the oldest son, with three younger brothers to tend. Even at this early age, there were many things I was being asked to do that had more importance in the world than my little song. And yet, for me this was probably the most significant thing I had ever done. Not only did it signal the value that music was to have in my life, but— perhaps of even more importance—I was being made aware that even in the midst of the demands of the world, I was also being invited to respond to what seemed to be the impractical and "useless" calls from within.

"There is something you find interesting, for a reason hard to explain," writer Annie Dillard says to us. "It is hard to explain because you have never read it on any page. You were made and set here to give voice to this, your own astonishment."

What I have come to see through my own life and those of others is that each life is given something, a question perhaps or a curiosity, one not yet fully formed, but one whose nature is so compelling that we are drawn to it like a gravity pull. We live in service of it, sometimes blindly following its trail, even if we are offered only a few subtle cues to guide our way. The trick, of course, for each of us is to discover how to follow the clues.

"The most demanding part of living a lifetime as an artist,"

Annie Dillard goes on to say, quoting the words of sculptor Annie Truitt, "is the strict discipline of forcing oneself to work steadfastly along the nerve of one's own intimate sensitivity."

What does it mean to follow the nerve of our own intimate sensitivity? What is it that has true heart and meaning in our life? Is there something that we can be steadfast about, something that so attracts our curiosity, interest, and passion that we are willing to stand with that above all else? Is it possible to uncover the doubts and uncertainties that so often disguise these mysterious attractions and curiosities with vague feelings of dissatisfaction and a busyness that dulls our senses and claims our lives?

For many years, I resisted these questions. "I am a pianist," I would say. "I don't know how to speak of this in words." I was content to simply sit at the piano, to let it be my oasis, a place to which I could retreat from the chaos and pain of the world. But life had other ideas. One evening, I sat in the Green Room in a small concert hall in New England. It was intermission. I had a few moments to plan the second half of the evening. Generally, I didn't submit program notes in advance, preferring instead to play through the music as I felt it, rather than try to force my program to fit some preset plan.

So, I was using this opportunity to sketch out some ideas on the back of an envelope before the second part of the evening began.

What about *Swallows in Space?* I mused to myself. No, just a minute, I played that one in the first set. . . . Well, okay then, how about *Aspen Summer*, that would be a good start, and then I could go on to . . . *Spring Song.* Suddenly, my throat became very dry. I had played all of these compositions in the first half of the evening.

No, that's impossible; how could I have? I said to myself.

Although I had played only a few concerts, I had never run short of music before. I knew I was a little nervous tonight, but did I play them that fast? My mind was racing. As soon as I noticed its rapid pace, I realized that perhaps I had. But there was no further time to waste trying to figure it out. The lights were flickering on the stage, and in a few moments, four or five hundred people would be returning to their seats in the hall. They would be expecting me to return to the stage as well. But I didn't want to go—I didn't have any more music left to play.

Slowly I walked across the stage and sat at the piano. My mind was foggy, but fortunately my voice was clear. I turned to look across the darkened hall. I was able to make out some faces in the front two rows, so I spoke to them. This relaxed me.

"People sometimes ask where the inspiration for my music comes from," I began. "I have sometimes wondered the same thing." As I talked, I surprised myself with how quickly I warmed to the task. What came to me to speak of were not so much theories or ideas, but stories, ones that spoke about my life and where the music had come from. What was so significant about the stories I chose to share was that I had forgotten that they were there. They were not the ones that I usually told. In fact, these had been so distant from my mind that I could no longer be sure that they were true.

Perhaps the stories that hold the most significance for us work this way. They are experienced and then forgotten. When they are recalled, they are no longer simply a part of our biography, but reveal how the mythic dimension of the universe is weaving itself into the fabric of our personal lives; details of time and place and chronology are overshadowed by the importance these stories hold in revealing the deeper meaning that is emerging as our lives unfold. Although the story itself may represent only a small moment in time, it shows that we are participants in a larger story, one that lives in us, but finds its origin in all that has gone before. When we speak of it, it is no longer just a memory, but a living presence: Our words carry the weight and conviction of our own experience; we have earned these stories—they are now in our blood. As we discover how to follow the stories' unfolding trail of meaning, we can appreciate how perfectly suited they are for us: They become our teachers, subtly and exquisitely revealing to us our next steps. Then we are complete within ourselves; no one else's knowledge is greater than our own.

After the concert, many members of the audience pulled me aside to tell me one of their own stories. The freshness and excitement in their words revealed to both of us that they also were sharing them for the first time. The stories offered a bridge, a means through which I could let my life merge with theirs, and theirs with mine.

How many of us, I wonder, are walking around with stories inside of us that we are unaware of? Stories that speak deeply of who we are, ones that are waiting urgently to be told. Our life is a story, Carl Jung once said, and our spirit needs to have this story in order for us to live. When our story is lost, he believed, the culture is lost as well.

How many of us remember, as children, being sustained by the stories that were shared under a dusty yellow light beside a freshly pulled-down bed? How often have we been spontaneously filled with feelings of wonder, joy, and tears as the story offered us, in its telling, a warmhearted and welcoming embrace of life? Perhaps that is why I have always loved to tell and to listen to stories. Some part of me dissolves away, and I stand naked in the essence of who I truly am. That was what had been significant for me that evening. In walking to the stage empty-handed, I had been given something. I was no longer playing an instrument, I *was* one. I had become a vehicle through which the deeper purposes and rhythms of life could be felt, and the longings of the heart revealed.

After that evening, I thought more deeply about my life as an artist. Maybe it was too easy to try to isolate myself from the larger community of which I was a part. "Artists are the antennae of the race," Ezra Pound once said. I began to see that my needs for privacy needed to be balanced with an awareness that the sharing of my music and stories might help to awaken the artist that is so often sleeping within each of us.

So, in addition to sharing the stories in concerts, I decided to write about them as well. But no sooner had I put the pen to page, than this short book grew from a few pages after the first week to five or six chapters a few months later. Outlining the stories had soon led to writing about piano playing, and this soon led to writing about creativity. And the topic of creativity, I realized, was larger than I had first envisioned. Within a short time, I felt a little like a fish trying to write about the sea.

In the meantime, somewhere in this process, the stories got lost, and so did the music. The subtle magic of that evening had been overridden by another part of my nature that was demanding that this project become bigger and better. In doing so, the stories that had first inspired it got left behind. And the piano that had been the source of the stories was put aside as well. It sat forgotten and untouched, it strings untuned, its surface buried in dust.

My office, on the other hand, was a flurry of activity. Mounds of paper, each page more dense than the other with theoretical expositions and quotations, filled my desk. The floor beside my chair was stacked high with drafts of chapters, each more labored and abstract than the last. Although the content of what I wrote was about creativity, the process by which I was writing was becoming anything but.

Finally, it was done. I passed it along proudly to a friend, an editor, for comment.

A month passed, then the editor and I met late one September afternoon. "What about your stories?" she said, by way of beginning. "I remembered how you described them to me when you first began to write. I always enjoyed them, but I don't see many of them here."

"Hmm . . ." I replied, feeling a little self-conscious. I had almost forgotten them. "I discarded most of them," I said defensively. "Why don't you just do some light editing on the rest."

She sat silent for a moment and then cleared her throat. "I liked them! If you want my honest opinion, I suggest that you include the stories—and discard the rest."

This was followed by a much longer silence. Slowly, the sun drifted behind a cloud. The birds that had sung merrily around us when we sat down to talk seemed to have gathered now in the far pasture. Their voices so full and rich a moment ago were now faint and distant.

"But the *rest* is 90 percent of the manuscript," I protested. "I can't just throw it out."

"Let the stories speak for themselves," she said. "Once you have put yourself back into this book, you won't need all the rest."

The following week, I reread the manuscript. She was right. Somewhere in the process, there had been a palace revolt. The part of myself that had helped me navigate through school essays, college honors papers, and a graduate dissertation had taken over the show. It was a voice that put more faith in concepts and theories than in direct experience and held a greater investment in showing off my competencies to the world than in revealing my vulnerabilities. It had little faith or patience with the poetic, uncertain, heartfelt, dreamy, imaginative parts of my nature. Though this mental intelligence may have helped me get good grades, it had little interest in revealing the deeper desires that lay within my heart. Yet it was my heart that came most to life when I sat at the piano, and, though its voice may often feel tentative, awkward, and unformed when first heard, it was from this part of myself that the words for this book must come.

My head was ready to push on and make the necessary corrections, but I was listening more to my heart now, and it was ready for a rest. It needed time and space to do its work. Although its rhythms might unfold more slowly, I trusted that the words that did flow from it would draw from a different inspiration, one that was free and independent of external stimulation and therefore more likely to be heaven-sent.

I also realized that I was writing in the wrong place. I had been working upstairs, and the piano was downstairs. It was *down* I needed to go if I were to truly write this book. So, I returned to the piano, tuned its strings, and dusted the keys. And as I experienced the joy of playing again, the purpose of this book became clear. It was about piano playing, but it was not about technique. It was about recognizing that our "artfulness," whatever form it takes, is neither a luxury nor something to distract us during our leisure time. Instead, it is an integral part of the whole of ourselves. It offers an insight into the tasks that we are here to fulfill; it provides a place of inner nourishment, a reminder that, no matter what life brings us, we can always come back to the well.

"Art," as author Laurens van der Post says, "is the guardian and maker of the chain," a window into our history, the means through which the original story can continue to unfold. The artistic impulse may be difficult to explain or understand, but when we deny its claims upon us, we are giving up on our lives as well. Our art is not only painting or sculpture or music, it is a vitality, an energy, a defining impulse, one that serves others and fulfills ourselves. It is the way through which we give form to our own imaginative life. For some, it is found in the alchemy of cooking or in listening deeply to another person. Others find it in providing compassionate care for another or in transforming an environment in a beautiful way. Whatever it is for us, it doesn't matter how good it is or how it compares to others, or even whether we are talented at it; if it brings us true joy, it is the purpose for which we came into being.

This impulse does not need to be found, for it is already preserved—it is simply through being open to the possibility of its presence that it is awakened. Once touched, we discover that there is another intelligence, one acquired not from books and schools that may rank our standing in the world but another, one that the Sufi poet Jelaluddin Rumi speaks of as:

. . . already completed and preserved inside you.
A spring overflowing its springbox. A freshness
in the center of the chest. This other intelligence
does not turn yellow and stagnate. It's fluid,
and it doesn't move from the outside to the inside
through the conduits of plumbing-learning.

This second knowing is a fountainhead
from within you, moving out.

Tapping into our creative impulse opens the doorway to this different kind of intelligence, one that is not concerned with improving our competence or filling our minds with facts, but rather that asks us to give a tangible form to some aspect of the unformed potential that has its roots in the invisible world. This is not a linear process that can be conveniently and willfully performed. It is an opening to a possibility and a knowing, one that rests deep within the heart of each of us. The music and images and words we construct reveal the means by which we are able to make sacred our own immediate and direct experience of ourselves and the world. There are no "have to's" here—whatever comes is where we start. Slowly we are drawn beyond the quantitative world into another more subtle place, one that expands our senses so that, as William Blake once said, we become like a "harp struck by the hand divine."

I have often found it difficult to speak of this imaginative realm. If there is a way of bringing language to this experience without diminishing it, I believe it is to be found and nourished through the sharing of stories and poetry and song. It has a kinship with animals and nature. It is more than the sentimental heart that we hear about in song lyrics. It is instead a vast and intimate intelligence that lives deep within our body, the only organ powerful enough to warm the sometimes cool and abstract workings of our mind. Yet it comes to us often in the lightest and smallest of touches, like the delicate sound of the wind rustling the leaves on a tree. Its presence is so subtle and so foreign to our thoughts that we often do not know that we have been touched at all.

We don't go to it, so much as we allow it to come to us. It does so in those moments when our hard-earned skills are transformed into an act of grace. It flows through us in a way that elevates our carefully crafted abilities into a work of art. "Life can't ever defeat a writer who is in love with writing," author Edna Ferber once said, "for life itself is a writer's lover until death." Each time we strike a piano key, lift a paintbrush, fire a kiln, dance with abandon, cook a beautiful meal, or write a poem, we are inviting the heart-felt intensity of the lover to come into our lives.

"You're a teacher, not a musician," a friend said to me one day. And, in some ways, he is right. In my profession as an educator and a communicator of ideas, I am engaged in a calling that could fill the entire span of my life. For fifteen years, I had enjoyed working with managers and employees, helping them transform their work units and organizations into learning communities. But the piano is my lover, who has taught me how to serve the field of ideas in an entirely different way. It has shown me how to risk stepping forward when I didn't know where that would lead; it has encouraged me to take that step even when I could not foresee how the step following that one would come. It has helped me see that though there may be a limit to the intelligence of the head, there is no limit to the intelligence of the heart. It has been a daily reminder that there is an inspiration inside each of us that will guide us whenever we give it space in which to breathe. All of this has transformed my teaching beyond anything that I could have ever foreseen.

Author Bruce Chatwin tells the story of how the aboriginal people of Australia had a songline, one in which the rise and fall of the melody line corresponded with the changing contours of the land. They had no map to guide their way in the wilderness, but they could feel the path unfold before them, step by step, so long as they remembered their song. I believe that each of us has our own songline, and when we listen to and trust the deeper impulses that inspire our actions, our world becomes a musical score. The awareness of something that is uniquely our own and that only we can do transforms our lives into song. The youngest joins with the oldest parts of ourselves; we feel a renewed connection with the first spirit of the earth, one that tells us to name our gifts and desires and bring new life to all that we meet.

Although this trip is ultimately our own to make, it is also the kind of adventure that welcomes company. Others may join, as participants perhaps, but, more important as midwives, willing to assist in the birthing of new creations along the way. Though our finished products may eventually pass away, our participation in this unfolding theater of collective human experience releases an energy that will go on to do its work in ways we cannot foresee. That's why, although making art in any of its forms is often considered self-indulgent, it may, in fact, be the most selfless of acts, because each step we take for ourselves is also one that we take for everyone else.

"But I have nothing to give," we might protest. To which Henry

David Thoreau replies: "The woods would be silent, if the best birds were the only ones that sang."

Birds don't sing constantly, but, when they do, they bring their entire being into the act. Perhaps this is what is being asked of us. To do what we love, to learn to do it well, and to not do it all the time. Even the smallest of acts is sufficient—we do not have to give up our life. At the same time, no one is exempt. In fact, it probably takes far more energy to resist singing our song than it does to let it be heard. No one can give life to this impulse but you, and no single human being can carry the song for us all.

This book is an invitation to let those songs be heard. To begin the journey and find your own way. The journey *is* the song. The spirit we bring to our work lingers on, regardless of the final result. Its lyric is found in the dreams and images that form us. "We are God's dream dreaming us," our ancestors once said. It was a dream that held them as they moved faithfully in the wilderness by day and grew in influence as they shared its meaning by the fire at night.

Our dreams have the power to hold us. They grow in meaning as their images are shared by the fire. It is time again for us to meet and talk. To explore our togetherness in a world that is in need of a new song to be sung. It is a time to speak of our collective longings without having to answer why, and to trust that there is a truth in the earth, one that we may have forgotten but that has not forgotten us. It is time to listen to a wisdom that perhaps can be heard more clearly when we are together than when we are apart.

Creating an imaginative life is to live an original one. It is a life that is respectful of the sometimes unreasonable and inexplicable impulses that originate from within; it is a life that finds its authority in its own experience, rather than conforming to that which has been passed on to us secondhand.

Though it is a life that may be planned, it is also an improvised life, one that seeks to find balance between the implicit power of our intentions and the beauty of those subtle and mysterious forces that seem to be forming us as we go.

Perhaps in listening to these forces, we will hear again the one song that holds it all, the one that reminds us that what is outside of us is inside of us as well, the one that says to us that we are the composers of our own experience and have the capacity to re-imagine the world. It's time to let our voices join in the creation of the great song, the one which reminds us that we are already all that we wish to become, the one that says finally that to reawaken the dream we have only to rest in ourselves; to love what we love, and feel what we feel. In so doing we will be guided by the silent intelligence that beats deeply within each of our hearts.

Dancing with the Animals

Last fall, I prepared for a concert by taking long walks in the country. I watched the black squirrels running furtively across the grass, gathering nuts among the leaves. Large flocks of wild geese rested and bathed in the frigid November waters. Soon they would resume their long flight south.

I love to feel the change in the seasons. To see my breath turn to mist as it evaporates in the cold, damp air. To feel the fleeting warmth of the summer sun as its weakening rays try to penetrate the rich and vivid canopy of changing leaves overhead, transforming the great old maples into a fiery red. I watch the dark gray clouds scudding quickly from horizon to horizon, parting only briefly to reveal patches of deep blue sky just beyond.

For many years, I lived in the middle of a large city. There, the noise of traffic and shrill cries of sirens colonized the silence. The polluted air muted the sky. I felt then as though I lived in a

giant dome, where the wind blew with less urgency, where the thunder and lightning lacked brilliance, and even the sunlight left the skin pale and lifeless.

Still, the city made up for these failings with other offerings. I sat late into the night in jazz clubs, baked in the heat at folk festivals, joined in street dances, listened mesmerized in hushed concert halls, and felt my ears go numb at rock concerts. But as impressive as this music was, eventually I was always drawn back to exploring the sounds that came from within. Sometimes I became frustrated with myself, thinking that perhaps it was time to take lessons again and learn how to play the piano properly. But I could not deny that each time I entered into a partnership with the instrument, rather than impose myself upon it, I was guided into spontaneous musical journeys that were sometimes peaceful and serene, at other times stormy, melancholy, poignant, magical, hopeful, and, occasionally, even heroic and wise.

There was a discipline here, but it had more to do with letting go into the notes; with feeling where they wanted to go; with directly experiencing the music, even when I didn't have a concept for it; with allowing myself to get lost, and savoring the infinite variety of ways I had for finding my way back—none of which was mentioned much in my piano lessons.

When I closed the music books, softened my vision, and waited upon the patterns of notes that emerged, something else breathed its life into the music, loosening the harmonic structures and forms that I had so carefully shaped. I didn't know who was playing the music then, but I didn't think it was me. During these times at the piano, I felt expansive inside, glowing in the fullness of knowing that in this moment in time, I was simply being myself, doing what I loved to do most.

Several years ago, my partner, Judy and I left the city and moved to the country. On this cold, blustery November day, I felt grateful that I no longer needed to use the music to transport me here. Now I could enjoy nature's unfolding patterns firsthand. As I watched the animals at play and the wind churning up the water close to shore, I appreciated, perhaps for the first time, how much the rhythms of the natural world inspired the music I loved to play.

Later, I shared this experience with a friend. As he listened, he pulled a poem from his desk.

"I thought you might enjoy this," he said.

The poem described a composer listening to her own work,

"the 'beast of sound caged' within the music bars."

Putting the poem down, he said thoughtfully, "You don't cage the animals when you play, do you? You dance with them."

His observation stopped me short for a moment. Although I had spent a good portion of my time on the piano bench, I had no language to describe how I played or what inspired it. When anyone asked, I was immediately at a loss for words. They were amused. I was a communicator in other parts of my life, but any questions about music were usually met with a shrug and a look of dismay. I realized that I did not know how to grasp, in words, these benevolent and mysterious forces that were so generously at my side when I played but over which I felt I had so little control. To speak of it too casually might dissipate the energy and perhaps violate a sacred trust.

But this image of dancing with the animals stayed with me. It offered an insight into an invitation I had received very early in life. It was one in which I was shown that, when I freely joined the animals in their play, I was also entering into the dance of life. It was a relationship of trust, but it was also a reminder. If I could keep alive my sense of wonder, of spontaneity, and of play, the instructions regarding which steps to dance would be shown to me along the way.

I was two when my aunt Elinor, who was only seven years older, first helped me onto the piano bench to watch her play. She was taking lessons and often practiced when I came to visit. I was captivated by her hands. How did she know which keys to press? Sometimes I would be cross-eyed, trying to follow her speeding fingers. Carefully, I watched her depress a key until it was out of sight. Then, I wondered where it went. I looked in the cracks between the keys, and a shiver ran up and down my back as I imagined what lay below. From storybooks, I knew that dragons and monsters lived in dark places, so I decided there must be dragons living *in* the piano!

The story of the troll that lived under the bridge was also very real for me. The troll used to catch and eat the billy goats as they walked nervously, in single file, across the narrow bridge to graze in the open field on the other side. The goats, knowing that the troll was underneath, would each take a deep breath before walking carefully onto the bridge and making their way slowly across.

I held my breath as my aunt depressed each of the white keys. In my mind, they were the goats, and as they disappeared from view, I waited anxiously for their return. When she played quickly, I could relax. They were now too fast for the troll. I knew from my storybooks that the dragons were wild. They moved silently in the shadows and they ate children. I didn't want to do anything to disturb them. So, when Elinor hit a wrong note or banged the keys in frustration, I drew back in fear. I anticipated that this noise would stir them, making them angry and bringing them out into the open, where they might notice me. Knowing how close they might be, a cold chill ran through me. I moved closer to my aunt for comfort. Though the piano fascinated me, it would be some time before I ventured too close to it on my own.

While I thrilled at these adventures, I was also filled with many questions. Where did the sounds come from, and why did she sometimes play the black notes and at other times the white ones? She often read from a book illustrated with pictures of animals— big black bears and rabbits with smiling faces filled the margins of the pages. There were birds as well, sitting high in the treetops, singing joyfully to each other and flying from branch to branch. These images expanded my ideas about what was in the piano. Behind the wood panels was another world—one of considerable mystery. The dragons must live in the bottom, in the dark caves. Just behind the keys and farther up lived the other animals, while the birds lived at the top. There was room here for everyone! *I* was safe on the piano bench!

I could relax now, knowing that it was the animals that created the sounds. Each time my aunt played, they danced; and their dancing created the music. When a wrong note happened, it was a dragon trying to catch one of the animals. Quickly, I surveyed the keys to be sure that none was missing. Phew! All of the animals were safe.

They were the magicians behind the music. After I figured this out, I wanted to enter this world and discover its secrets. Before, I was content to watch my aunt's hands, but now I was ready to join the animals. I was ready to play!

My aunt helped me onto her lap and carefully guided my hands along the keyboard. Supporting my palm with her hand, she helped me press each finger into one of the keys. Gradually, I touched all of the notes, both black and white. I was so excited that I could not restrain myself. I hit a handful of notes with my palm and listened keenly as they reverberated loudly around the room. I freely challenged the dragons to show themselves. Patiently, she took my hand again, and we walked up and down the instrument. When the notes sounded, I smiled; the animals were saying hello. I felt welcomed into this strange and wonderful land.

I loved the texture of the keys. They felt smooth and cool to my touch. I liked to feel the edges and the narrowness of the black keys and watched closely to see how they slipped down between the white ones. I like the musty smell of the wood, and its strength. The piano towered well above my head, even when I was sitting on the bench. Everything about this world at the piano made me feel like I belonged here. Soon, I was playing with both hands, delighting myself with the contrasts and fullness of sound. The opportunity to freely explore was an invitation to let my imagination go wild. I came to appreciate that the universe just behind the keys was mine and that the furry animals would dance to my touch. I growled, and sang, and walked the keys from top to bottom. I was loud, soft, tender, angry, and sad. Here at the piano, I was developing a vocabulary of feeling and nuance that was broader and more precise than words.

Sometimes, my aunt would join me. As she played, I placed my own hands gently over hers. Here, I could feel her movement and rhythm, a sensation that instinctively found its way into my own playing. The piano was my playground. I gladly brought the animals out of their cages and danced with them. But while I learned some of the piano's secrets, I retained a healthy respect for its mysteries. I was reluctant to ask too many questions for fear that, in the words of J. R. R. Tolkien, "the gates should be shut and keys be lost."

And yet I discovered that on the days when the animals were not there, it was the questions that brought them back. They kept me open and fluid in a way that the answers did not. It was when I became too concerned with bringing things to a conclusion that everything came to a stop. Then I was on my own. There was no dance.

When I approached the piano with an inquiring mind, the

animals spoke back with a playful one, encouraging me to explore all of the possible ways that a note might sound. And because this conversation came less from duty and more from fun, I could engage in it for hours. But, when my demands for certainty intruded upon this space, or a voice inside insisted that I be told the one right way, the animals became bashful and ran for cover. And, once gone, they might not return all day.

As I lived the questions, there was nothing to defend or explain. And I learned that the discoveries that held the most meaning at the piano often came obliquely. When I pushed too hard for an answer, it often turned out to be the answer for the wrong thing. As I learned to follow my curiosities, it was the beauty I found in the sounds that became my most reliable guide.

Many years have passed since my glimpse of those animals on the pages of the music book. But now, as I help others learn to suspend their long-cherished opinions and beliefs in order to connect with their deeper truth within, I find that I am dancing with them again.

"Where shall we find the way to heaven?" the Apostles asked Christ one day.

"Follow the birds, the beasts, and the fish," he answered, "and they will lead you in."

The way in for me has involved taking the relationship I have been exploring at the piano and bringing that into the rest of my life as well. Is it possible, I ask, to be a knower, confident in the knowledge that I can play each note exactly as I have before, and, at the same time, to be a learner, open and curious about the many possible ways that a note might go? Can I learn to accept my certainties and at the same time live broadly enough to include the inexplicable and the mysterious into my life, accepting that I can be a competent performer one moment and in the next feel carried along by an impulse that offers me little guidance as to where the music might go? How willing am I to engage with those more diffuse dimensions of life—of dreams and images and possibilities—ones that are so close to the roots of our existence but which have, as Rainer Maria Rilke says, ". . . been so crowded out of life that the senses with which we could have grasped them are atrophied?"

The dance is always found in the new. It comes to us through engaging the world with a beginner's mind, one willing to encounter, with an open and inquiring ear, even the familiar as that which has not yet been seen, or heard, or known. The wisdom of the animals cannot penetrate through our habits or routines. When we become too enmeshed or established in the old, life's mystery can no longer reach us; our eyes grow dull and can no longer see or enjoy the magic in the world. It is when we are ready to receive that impulse, one which wants to express itself from within ourselves, that we are in an immediate connection with life itself.

"We have no reason to mistrust the world," Rilke reassures us. We have been equipped by life, for life; and that life is so much a part of us that if we were to be still for just a moment, the trees and plants and animals that seem so separate from us most of the time would feel like they were a part of us as well. It is this sense of merging into a larger life that I experience when I step into the new. When I place the source of life outside of myself, it is easy to feel restricted; I feel lifeless and dull. But when I follow what is flowing from within and trust it, I have never been abandoned; the well is always full.

"No traps or snares are set about us," Rilke reassures us. "There is nothing that should intimidate or worry us, we are set down in life as in the element with which we best correspond." We are here to encounter life in all of its forms, even if that means holding onto what seems most difficult, because even that will, in time, transform itself into a trusted and faithful friend. However we choose to live, he invites us to live it as broadly as we can. The nature of this dance has been difficult to articulate in my teaching, so I have often chosen to let the piano be my voice instead.

"I am going to play a composition from memory," I say to seminar participants. "But as I do so, I am also going to remain open to the possibility of something else emerging. If it does so, I would like to follow that to see where it might go. Close your eyes and listen to the piano. See if you feel or hear a shift in the energy in the music and notice if your relationship with yourself changes as well."

I often feel vulnerable doing this in front of others. I don't know how the music will come or what it might reveal. Part of the difficulty is that when I play the piano in an improvisational way, it is different from how I have been trained. I cannot master this practice and force it to submit to my will. Instead, in order to feel the flow of the music, it helps if I am willing to enter into the process in a spirit of play rather than work. This is where the animals have been of great help. It has involved freeing myself of any illusions regarding how the music should be played, and instead allowing myself an openness to see and appreciate the reality of each moment for what it is. When I do this, I discover that the flow is always there, like an impulse that comes in through the heart rather than the head. I cannot think my way into it. On the contrary, each time I do it, I need to find new ways of tricking my mind to relax. The mind, I have learned, is very clever. As soon as it recognizes that it's entering territory where it is not in charge, it becomes very protective. It quickly begins inventing reasons to stop, because it does not want to let go.

One way around it is to stay close to my own feelings of vulnerability, to lean ever closer and hold onto that fine line of uncertainty without falling off. Then I experience a shift in my playing, one in which I feel both humbled by the power of the music and expansive at the same time. My eyes soften, my ears feel as big as the piano, my fingers feel like they have a life of their own, and a profound stillness settles in the room.

When it comes time to talk, participants notice how much more space there is between their words than there was before. We all feel wiser than we were. There is less need to try to over-refine our ideas or argue our points of view; there is a sense that a powerful presence has joined us in the room, one that communicates through silence, perhaps, more than through words. Our use of language changes as well. Our conventional use of words, in the literal sense, seems inadequate. We search instead for words that are congruent with our sense of the moment, ones that give honor and dignity to our own immediate, firsthand experience. These words are found more through the language of poetry, metaphor, and story.

"So much of my knowledge is secondhand," someone says. It comes from what I hear, from teachers, newspapers, television, and books. The music is a reminder that there is another voice inside that wants to speak. This voice is not interested so much in the careful formulation or defense of opinions and beliefs. Instead, it is a spontaneous impulse, one that flows from a desire to speak from a source of truth that is both immediate and, perhaps because it has not been formed in advance, more heartfelt.

As I listened, I remembered a conversation with a friend from many years before. He was describing how he had almost crash-landed a small plane he was piloting one afternoon. "You must have been terrified!" I said, with feelings of deep care and concern.

"It was the most exhilarating moment of my life!" he said in response. "The terror came later, after I got the plane safely back to the field." As we talked further, he pointed out an interesting thing. The fear and terror he felt seemed to be more a reflection of what others were feeling that day. When he tried to speak about what his actual experience had been, it seemed that no one wanted to hear. As he talked, I wondered how often the authority of our own immediate experience is lost because it does not conform to what we are expected to feel.

It was the inner authority of this experience that was emerging as we spoke that day. People gradually began revealing a depth of insight and wisdom that went beyond what they thought they believed. It came not from any one person, but flowed through us, very much as the music did, and was amplified by the growing sense of connection that was forming in the group. "I don't have time for this," one businessman said impatiently as he joined with us that morning. But by the end of the day, he was so convinced of its importance that he had time for nothing else.

"We take so little time to simply sit together and talk about what is really true for us," another person said. And yet the truth of the words that originate from within ourselves is so important. For our choice of language shapes our beliefs, and our beliefs shape our experience of the world.

I am grateful that the teachings the animals have offered me over the years can also be shared. For in our hearts we are all hunters, engaged in an act that has been a part of us from the beginning of time. It is to be obedient to that instinctive dimension of our experience, which is to not merely follow but to deliberately stalk that which has meaning for us, to imprint upon life our own unique spirit based on what we find to be most immediate, direct, and true. That search began on my aunt's knee, and it is the same search that I am engaged in now. No matter what our calling, ultimately we are all artists when we allow ourselves to be the instruments through which we find this truth in our life. Yet too much thinking about it can shut our hearts down; we must engage in this process lightly, allowing whatever conclusions we form to be like shadows that dance in the wind.

As the years pass, I am still learning to take the dance inside. It lives in me now, just as I live in it. When I am connected to it, I cannot repeat myself; even the familiar notes at the piano sound fresh and new. There are risks in living an imaginative life; it is easy to lose the path, and not every creation may be a work of art.

"But what if I fail?" someone once asked. Upon hearing this question, I realized that my only real failures have been in hearing the call from within and failing to act. Perhaps the deeper question is: Whom and what do I serve? And then to notice what is emerging in response to the question and live my life in obedience to that. Yet action is difficult when we discover that we have left behind the companions who have invited us to the dance. As a child, I sometimes imagined that I heard the animals tapping on my bedroom door at night, inviting me to come downstairs to play. Who is knocking on your door now? Who or what is inviting you to play? What is emerging now that you cannot deny—the urge to paint, to write, or to simply sit by a tree all day? Will it take a rain check, or do you get only one chance? And what is the source of that voice inside that is telling it to go away?

One thing has become clear to me: Once we open the channel, we will remember that there is a place of embodied knowing within us, a capacity to think with our hearts as well as our heads. This is the place that the animals have always known. We are all an integral part of the dance of creation. When I let the music play me, I am one step closer to the Garden than I was before. In this moment, I am no longer playing the music. In the words of T. S. Eliot, "I *am* the music, as long as the music lasts."

Casey on the Bench

"Who was your first piano teacher?" someone once asked.

And just as I was about to reply with a name of my first teacher, I remembered that there was another one long before that. He was a brown and white springer spaniel called Casey.

Casey would have been my name if my father had had his way. But my mother refused, so a pact was made—my name would be Michael, and later we would get a dog and call him Casey. So, as I held this wiggling warm ball of fluff in my arms as we left the kennel, it was love at first sight, partly because of the way he was licking my face, but mostly because he was named Casey and not me.

Piano playing involves the mastery and organization of notes and chords, of rhythm and timing, of being familiar with the written score. The time would come when I would try to keep all of this in my head. But playing also involves the movement of energy, feeling the flow and allowing my hands to lead the way. To master this, I had to follow my nose.

This is where Casey was my teacher. The wagging of his tail, the stretch of his body, the graceful leap over the tops of bushes—these were the images that inspired my own playing. He was so natural in his movements and never held anything back; I was sure that if I could carry this same instinct to my playing, I couldn't make any serious mistakes.

What I noticed most was the alertness with which he brought his attention to the world around him. Not only to its sights and sounds, but to its smells. Often he became riveted, feet braced, body trembling, his nose stuffed deep inside some unremarkable clump of leaves or grass, sitting unobtrusively near a large maple tree. It was the same one I passed by three or four times a day. But for Casey, an entire world existed beneath these leaves. In these brief moments, Casey was no longer the soft cuddly spaniel that curled around my legs at night. Deep in his heart beat the ancient blood memory of the hunter stalking his prey. He stepped slowly and deliberately, searching carefully for the fleeting scent that claimed his absolute and total concentration.

Now when I sit at the piano, I also stop for a moment to sniff the air. It is usually enough to get me started. Musical ideas often begin this way. There is no path, just a cluster of ambiguous and unformed ideas. To explore where they want to go, I have to bring all of my senses into play and let them lead the way. Slowly and deliberately, I stalk the keys, listening to each note and searching, my ears stretched far beyond my head for just the right tonality that will capture the meaning of the sound that I want to convey.

Sometimes, I intentionally go to the piano with no particular idea or design in mind. Instead, I want to see what my fingers will do when they contact the keys. When my mind tries to divert my attention by saying, "This isn't very good," or, "I'm wasting my time," I'm reminded that Casey approached his world of flowers, trees, cats, balls, fence posts, old moldy boards, bugs, dead fish, and the mailman with equal enthusiasm and appreciation. These were the little things that held his fascination. He showed me that the entire world is there for us to enjoy, when we don't have any judgment in mind.

Casey's world and mine parted company each fall, about the third week of school. His flowers continued to bloom joyfully in the sun, mine now lay flattened and pressed in plastic. The frogs that leaped in front of his nose were now packed tightly in jars, preserved for my careful examination. My world became a greenhouse in which everything could be carefully controlled, but Casey's was a weed patch where everything could grow. I was saddened to think that while he remained a full participant in his world, I had become a spectator in mine.

It was only when I returned to the piano, closed my eyes, and set my fingers on the keys, that the world as I had remembered it came to life again. As I filled the room with the sounds I loved to hear, I realized that I lived in two worlds. One was full of the facts and theories and concepts that I was learning at school. These were the ones that I was told I must master to get good grades and ensure my standing in the world. For many around me, this was their only world. But for me, there was another. It lay mysterious and unformed, concealed safely among the shadows of the leaves and grass that Casey knew so well. It wasn't concerned with filling my head like pouring water into an empty bowl. Instead, it was a "knowing" on the inside, which said to me that I was already filled.

It was not always easy. School was teaching that the world belonged to me. It was my place to push hard, if need be, and impose my ideas with bold determination. But when I did this at the piano, there was only struggle; there was no flow. Frustrated, I would step away from the instrument, sometimes for days or weeks at a time. But, eventually, I always returned. I noticed how Casey always seemed to be so at ease in the moment, so at home in the universe, and so complete within himself, that I eventually let down my guard. I learned again to relax into the keys and waited once again for Casey to be my guide. So long as I approached the instrument in a spirit of openness and play, I was never alone. But when I became too serious or filled with thoughts of self-importance, Casey stayed away.

Casey eventually passed away, but when I sit at the piano, his spirit is always close by. Poet Mary Oliver says:

> A dog can never tell you what she knows from the
> smells of the world, but you know, watching her, that you know
> almost nothing.

At school, I was being told that the world was at my disposal, that it was here for my convenience and control. But Casey reminded me that it was the other way around. He wasn't here for my convenience any more than were the rain or the trees or the wind. He was here to remind me that there was another place from which my knowing could come. And the knowing he had to speak of had to do with love. He was so unconditional in his giving of it, as he ran and leaped across the open fields or pounced on a clump of pines in the woods, that I couldn't help but respond. His presence is in the music now. He is a living reminder of this simple truth each time I sit and play.

And while the world continues to fill my mind with facts that I must repeat from memory, Casey reminds me that, at the piano, it is in the forgetting that I find the key. Each time I practice this, I feel that I have stepped from the safety of dry land and dropped into the mystery of the sea. Here, I am no longer so concerned with goals or outcomes or the approval of others, or with how things are supposed to be. It is through not only tolerating but actively embracing the doubt and uncertainty, finding my plans for the day dissolve and beginning again with a blank page, sensing what was absent as well as what was there, that I know I am where I should be. In the absence of familiar patterns, my senses come to life, every note sounds fresh and new, and my playing takes on a new sensitivity. There is no end to it; each moment is both full and also incomplete.

When I play from this place, there is nothing abstract in my work. It doesn't matter if the music is simple or complex, so long as I listen closely to what I am doing. Then each note is played, not in an atmosphere of judgment, but in a spirit that remains true to the affections of my heart. The technique comes naturally then. My fingers seem eager to cooperate, actively searching for ways of executing what it is I want to play. If it is too much, I rest for a while. There is no need to punish them or force them to conform to my will.

The notes and chords are like food; they nourish me. For Casey, the world *was* food. Each object was carefully appraised to determine whether it was good enough to eat. This was kitchen work. For me, the piano is never located too far from the stove. I love to taste the music, to savor its sounds, to let the ideas simmer and cook for a while. I not only listen to the music, I digest it. When deeply engaged, I notice that my mouth is chewing the notes just as my fingers are playing them. And while I am shaping the music, it is changing me. All of the ingredients come together here, to be transformed quietly, without much need for noise. When I step away from the piano, I know that I am not the same person as the one who first sat down on the bench.

At school, I was being instructed in how to take the mystery out of the world. With Casey, I was learning how to put it back in. It involves, as Novalis says, "giving to the common an elevated meaning . . . and to the known the dignity of the unknown."

How do we put the mystery and magic back into our lives? Who is the enchanter who might open our heart to love? How can we creatively participate in the world in ways that might elevate our lives and give dignity to the unknown? How can we learn to engage in a dialogue with the lesser known parts of ourselves?

"But I am not an artist," some might say. "What do I know of magic and mystery and the unknown—and do I have to buy a dog?"

Whenever we are engaged in a dialogue or conversation with our world—whether with a person, a dog, a tree, or the part of us that feels uncreative, that is afraid to paint or dance—if there exists the possibility that we might be changed through this experience, then we are involved in a creative act. When the artist is alive in any person, artist and teacher Robert Henri says, "whatever his kind of work may be, he becomes an inventive, searching, daring, self-expressing creature . . . he disturbs, upsets, enlightens. Where those who are not artists are trying to close the book, he opens it, he does not have to be a painter or sculptor to be an artist, he can work in any medium . . . he simply has to find the gain in the work itself, not outside it."

Creation is life affirming. This is what I was destined to learn and what Casey came into the world to give. He was an adventurer; each day he made his rounds, discovering, in his examination of even the most familiar objects, entirely new things. And I'm grateful in knowing that I am offering back something of the gift that Casey came to give. There is no place to get to, or to do, or to be. It is found in the appreciation we hold for the music, for creation, and for trusting that it, and life itself, is its own reward.

Wild Horses on the Plains

One afternoon a few years ago, I was playing the piano for a group of children. After one of the pieces, I stopped and asked them what images the music brought to mind.

"Wild horses!" said Jimmy emphatically.

"What?" I said. I thought, perhaps, I had heard him incorrectly.

"Wild horses!" he said again. "There were a bunch of them, beautiful and black, galloping across the open plains."

His response was absolute. There was no doubt in his mind about what he had seen in the music. His response also animated the group, and they shared with me other images they had seen.

But the image of wild horses stuck in my mind. That was a new one. Later that day, I played for myself. I was curious to see if some of the images that came to me might be the same.

As I played, I remembered the birthday years ago when I received a boxed set of toy soldiers. They were accurate replicas of a regiment of eighteenth-century British riflemen. Each tin soldier had been carefully painted in immaculate detail, with shiny black boots, a red tunic, and white knickers. Carefully, I arranged them on the living room rug. Soon after this, I received a second set. This time it was a horse-mounted regiment.

On Saturday afternoons, I went to the store and pressed my nose hard against the window. In front of my eyes were box upon box of miniature reproductions open for display. It took only a moment for my imagination to set to work. In an instant, they were transported from the confines of their cardboard prisons to the open fields of battle, where they belonged. Amid the imagined noise and dust, the colorful regiments marched into position, their bright banners snapping in the wind. Now as the cannon wagons were being wheeled and pushed onto the high hills, I set my own musical score. These were not just "piano" sounds that I created. They included the fanfares of a trumpet or the insistent beat of a bass drum. The scenes I was creating in my mind touched the larger and more heroic dimensions of life. Now I wanted the music to do the same.

One afternoon, my friends joined me on the living room rug. Together, they brought out their miniature soldiers and joined them with mine. Now we could re-create what I had so often imagined in my head. After several hours of thought and preparation, we were set to begin. I sat poised on the piano bench, my hands raised like a baton, waiting for the signal to play.

"*A duh de duh!*" one of them cried out, so that all the neighborhood could hear. Within a second, my hands dropped onto the high notes. The trumpet fanfare had begun. Then I set the drum on the low notes. The soldiers began their slow and steady march onto the open field. The drums and trumpets continued to herald the advancing columns. After a time, there was silence. Now the only sounds were the banners flapping in the strengthening wind. The horses became restless and uneasy, their thickly muscled necks straining against the black leather harnesses, their hooves kicking up loose dirt underfoot.

Then the first cannon sent its missile across the dull, clouded sky. I set my thumbs into the high notes and slid down the keyboard landing with a deep, resonant thud into the bass. Another cannon shot was fired, and I dropped into the lower notes once again. Quickly, the battle grew in intensity. In its midst, I was the conductor and the performers, my fingers bouncing up and down the keyboard, over high notes and low, white notes and black; nothing escaped the frantic rush of sound that emitted from the instrument.

As I played, another dimension of sound welled up unexpectedly from inside the piano and burned through my fingers. In that moment, I was no longer watching the battle—I was in it. The soldiers, the horses, the music, and I were all one and the same. There was no more pianist and no more piano. In this undefended moment of free flight, something changed in my body and God slipped in.

As soon as my mind noticed, God slipped back out again. But in that instant, I had experienced a moment of magic, a moment of unselfconsciousness, when I forgot myself and let go of control. I tried to recapture it, but what had seemed so natural a moment before was now impossible to re-create . . . or to forget.

Slowly, the soldiers withdrew, battle weary now, their soiled banners ripped and tattered as they carried their comrades from the field. The wind blew strong. I played a series of low notes in the minor keys and then let these drift off into silence.

"Wheew!" I said quietly to myself when it was over. "What was *that?*"

I watched now as my friends wrapped their soldiers carefully in tissue and packed them neatly into their boxes. But while everything appeared neat and orderly in their world, something had just popped out of mine. And as soon as I tried to analyze it, it was gone.

I felt a mixture of exhilaration and fear. In that "unattended moment" I had faced what T. S. Eliot describes as that "awful daring of a moment's surrender." Having once experienced this moment, I could feel more clearly when I was in it and when I was not. I learned to recognize when I'm trying to force the music into a performance or will it to conform to my plans. It feels labored then, as if I am playing on top of the keys rather than inside of them. I know, then, that I've lost it. I've gotten in my own way.

Gradually, however, as I got older, I trusted that these moments would come to me so long as I remained open to their possibility. They came by grace, and this grace came by learning. What I learned mostly was to practice what Rilke speaks of as a "carefree letting go of oneself, not a caution, but a wise blindness."

Cultivating a "wise blindness," however, was no simple undertaking. It involved developing a capacity for seeing things peripherally, or broadening my attention so that what was located at the edges of my perception became as important as what lay at the center. To do this, I had to learn to see with my ears. Slowly, I discovered that as I listened to the world, there no longer existed clear distinctions between foreground and background. There was simply a multilayered field of sound. As I immersed myself in this field, the musical ideas that came to me multiplied as well. I became fascinated with the question of whether it is possible to live "nonfocally," that is, to move in the world with a porous attention, one capable of attending to many stimuli at once, of hearing with my ears but also allowing these sensations to penetrate through my skin. How can I explore the infinite ways that a composition might go? Is it possible to not personalize it, to relax my attachment to maintaining a separate and discrete identity in order to join with the ongoing processes of creation of which I am a part? And if I am to do so, how do I begin?

These questions were drawing me into an emerging field of practice, a place in which I explored how to bridge these visible and invisible worlds. This involved taking time each day to play something new at the piano. What was wanted from me was something more than the tried and true. When I played a piece exactly the same way as I had before, my back began to ache, my eyes grew heavy, and my body felt like it wanted to sink to the floor. I shared very little with my friends of what I wrote during this time; in fact, when I listened closely to what I was playing, my critical mind was quick to step in and suggest that my dreams of a musical career might be a serious mistake. But my instincts told me to stay. This was not a time for establishing technical competence, but an opportunity to deepen my capacity; playing so awkwardly served to chip away some of my preoccupations with my own self-importance. Engaging in an activity that offered so few tangible rewards was a humbling act.

I was learning to practice as if *I* were being played. It was an act of preparation, an acknowledgment that although I could not create this experience on demand, I could tell whoever was listening that I was here, a willing participant ready to receive it if it came again. Perhaps the next time I could stay with the intensity a little longer without tensing up and pushing it away.

To find this in the music, I had to find it within myself. The intensity of one moment's surrender could not be stretched further unless my body could contain it. And while my thoughts often turned to how things might be in the heavenly realms, holding this energy also meant learning to keep my feet firmly on the floor. For many years, I played only the notes on the upper end of the piano, particularly those above middle C. I was drawn to finding how to create a lightly articulated sparkle in the high notes. The lower tones were too heavy, round, and dark. I didn't want to bother with them. But the energies that flowed through me so forcefully that day are not interested in how things have been before: They are always drawn toward the new; they stretch us upward and downward at the same time.

None of these steps happens quickly. Integrating the lower tones and minor notes into the music, and into my life, has taken many years and goes on still. In fact, it goes on by itself—the light and the dark, the upward and the downward, the over and the under—all seek and find a natural union when we don't interfere. Too often our impulse is to resist this union, to narrow ourselves down and make ourselves invisible in order that these unpleasant dimensions of life might pass us by. But our creations ask the opposite of us. They demand nothing less than our full-bodied, open-hearted response to life. Yet they cannot be called up on demand. It was only through practicing as though they were present that I created a welcoming home to which they might come.

Author Mary Catherine Bateson tells a wonderful story about a foreign correspondent's interview with a young Japanese woman during one of the World War II studies on Japanese culture. The journalist made a comment to her about Japanese respect for the father. "Oh, no," said the young woman, "in Japan we do not respect the father." The interviewer was flabbergasted, all his expectations contradicted. "You see," she said with the most delicate emphasis, "we *practice* respect for the father in case we someday find someone who deserves that respect."

Our practice prepares us for the experience. I can learn to be the rain and to be the wind, and to play music as if it were flowing like a rippling brook, but it is arrogant to believe that I can go to it directly, for it does not belong to me; I simply labor in good faith. Practice prepares me, it deepens my capacity so that when the moment does comes, I am ready: I am water, I am fire, the music has entered my body, it is flowing in my hands, I can feel it in the keys.

In practice, talent and preferences may take us off track. Talent tempts us to take shortcuts, whereas yielding to our preferences often means that when we no longer like what we are doing, we stop. Practice asks us to simply stay with the practice. It is often only through repetition that the invisible is made visible; random combinations of notes and chords emerge almost imperceptibly into a coherent shape, and a composition with which I had no relationship at the start begins, over time, to flow from my heart. "Artists fall in love with their work," Mary Catherine Bateson says, "at the point where it must be left alone." For me, this is the moment when the work is giving more back to me than I am giving to it. It is as if the act of creation sets loose an invisible field of energy that infuses my work. I can't touch it directly, but through engaging in my work, I create the experience, and in the experience, there is the possibility of this field touching me. To be touched for just one moment makes the entire process worthwhile. And although I may often feel the temptation to push the process, because nothing is happening and I fear feeling bored, it results only in frustration. The field of possibility has its own timetable. I have simply to walk the same path over and over again, always being open to discovering the new in the old, and trusting that it is in the cultivation of this state of willing obedience that I am engaging in the great work.

What, in your own life, is your current field of practice? What do you need to let go of within yourself, in order to provide a welcoming home to which it could come? What are the images that ignite your imagination and expand your field of possibilities? How do you find your own way in?

The way, for me, was through stories. It was the images and adventures from books and records that stimulated my auditory senses and nourished my playing. I imagined a group of people circled around the piano, speaking of journeys that circled and spiraled and curved back on themselves. The stories created an atmosphere in which I could walk the same path over and over again. The story was the journey. It transported me to distant places in geography, space, and time. I rode bareback with the Indians as they hunted buffalo on the open plains. I joined in the poetic songs the cowboys sang as they sat by their fires on cold, still, starlit nights. I drifted on a raft down the Mississippi and ex-plored dark mysterious caves with Tom Sawyer and Huck Finn.

Often, at school, I felt inferior when standing in the face of the lofty ideas or accomplishments of others. I cared little for what words symbolized or meant; it was the atmosphere and rhythm the words evoked that I searched for. I looked forward to the silence of the evenings, when my mind could free itself from the bondage of literal thinking and I could soak in the sound of words again. I listened for the clopping of horses' hooves on gravel by a rushing stream. I felt the rise and fall of the high-masted ships as they were carried along by great swells on a stormy sea. I was calmed by the silence on a high pasture and the whisper of wind through the pines. I loved to hear the crackling of a fire on a clear, cold night on the plains, and the noise of wind and rain rushing against a windowpane.

These impressions came to me much as the music did, float-ing in from the periphery of my conscious attention. And upon reading the same story a second or third time, even more sounds came into play. The facts and theories that narrowed my thinking dissolved under the flickering rays of a candle by my bed. When I opened my books, my imaginary landscape leaped into life. I stepped beyond the limits of my day-to-day experience; the world around me lent itself to more than one interpretation. In the words of Thoreau, I was learning to become "extravagant" again.

And of all the images that passed through the pages, there were two that stood the test of time. One was walking among wildflowers on steep, winding paths toward the high mountain pasture lands with Heidi. The other was riding a wild black horse across the plains.

I sat confidently on the back of this wild black horse, feeling his power and strength beneath me as he stood at the edge of a high place from which I could see mile upon mile across the open plains. This was the free spirit that carried me forward toward adventures I could not foresee. The wind and rain stung my face; the elements nourished and stimulated my senses. Knowing that I was safe and secure on his back, I was free to leave myself behind.

While riding this great black horse, I was also living the life of every hero I had ever known. I had a power here, one that was capable of making all things better, of riding in aid of all those I found to be in difficulty, of defeating those that held others in adversity, even while acknowledging the crowds who lined the long, winding roads that I traveled and who cheered me along.

Now, when I sit on the piano bench, I feel this black horse sturdy and strong beneath me. I grip the reins lightly but firmly in my hands. The flow I feel beneath my fingers is more important than any of the burdens or expectations that may try to weigh me down. And when I am really feeling connected to it, it just goes on and on. Music is the language of the imagination, the sounds dancing beneath my fingers, its themes emerging and dissolving into ever-changing forms. The adventure that I welcomed here was not in trying to memorize the notes but in not knowing what was to come.

When a friend observed that I was playing the piano with only half my body, it was the image of the wild horse that helped me find my legs again. Feeling the strength of its strong hooves beneath me reminded me that the passion and idealism that nourished my heart did not come from my head, but rather emerged from the earth and came up through the soles of my feet.

Bringing to life these forgotten images from childhood can help to uncover layers of adult conditioning. It offers the possibility of introducing into our practical lives some source of ancient wisdom that can animate and energize us. These energies, however, are often chaotic at first. There was a time when I played only dissonant music at the piano. Upon hearing it, more people left the room than entered it. A friend in an introductory art class, upon being asked by the teacher to paint trees, painted three of them. But because she did not like painting trees, each one she painted was broken—and black. Those hours of playing dissonant music prepared me to accompany modern-dance classes, a wonderfully rich experience that led directly to my finding my own musical voice. For my friend, those black and broken trees connected her to her own lifelong desire to paint—and her fear of doing so. Three months later, she enrolled in a fine-arts program at a local college and now she is painting and drawing full-time.

"The universe may be subtle," Albert Einstein once said, "but it is not malicious." The manner in which these energies enter into our life may be troublesome and even scary at first, but, in time, we learn that they have our larger interests at heart.

Jimmy had seen this ancient wisdom in the form of the wild horses. He reminded me that there is a wild part of our nature that refuses to be tamed. It is found in the images and stories and dreams that form us. It speaks of where we have come from, what is living in us now, and why our actions are sometimes governed more by a sense of inner necessity than choice. What remains wild in your life? Is there something that wants to become visible, something that can't quite fit into the existing structure of your world? Is there a new story emerging, one that holds within it an inner necessity to act, one that can no longer be ignored? If you took hold of its reins, where would it lead? The stories I loved were not only in the books I read, they were also in me. And the world would be incomplete without my living it.

Each of us has a story living in us. For some, it unfolds in an ongoing, continuous, and understandable way. It flows through them so naturally that they don't know that it's there. For others, it may include setbacks, detours, accidents, and deep loss. Perhaps an improvised life is like this; by making it up as we go along, we become more sensitive to following the subthemes that are not so obvious. But through acknowledging that we don't know which ideas may prove relevant, even those that result in dead ends in the short term may lay the groundwork for later success.

Each story carries the seeds of greatness in it, not so much because of the fame or success it may bring, but because it is no one else's story but our own. To resist living out our stories would be like trying to pretend that there is no wild horse in our lives. But it can be contained naturally when we orient our living around being attentive to what is appearing in the moment, trusting its intentions, and letting our field of practice be what we love.

When we tell our stories, we discover that those experiences that once seemed so private and personal are in fact most universal. They are shared by us all. Perhaps there is only one story, one in which we each play our individual part. Living out our part of the story is our life's work, and, in the end, we are asked to bring our enacted story back to the waters. "What have we loved and what have we learned," we are asked. In response, we offer our stories with all of the dignity that they deserve. Our imperfections, our loves, and our lessons are given back to the origins from which they came. They merge together within the deep well of collective human experience, a place where there is no beginning and no end.

Meeting the Dragon

Several years had passed since I first met the dragons that lived in the dark cavities of the piano cabinet. Eventually, I came to believe that they had simply been a reflection of my childhood fears. But I have since learned that dragons don't really go away. Instead, they are like great magicians who are able to constantly reinvent themselves in new and ever more intimidating forms. When they came to visit when I was a bit older, they did so, not as dark and mysterious shapes moving in the evening shadows beneath the piano keys, but dressed in the cloak of piano lessons, ready to torment me during the bright light of day.

Each week, I played scales and learned notation under the careful scrutiny of my music teacher. She watched the execution of each note with careful vigilance. She seemed capable of catching wrong notes even before my finger touched the key. How was I to preserve my natural and spontaneous relationship with the piano when I was constantly being stopped and reminded of the need for proper hand positions and correct fingering? I was in despair. From time to time, I tried to show her how I played my own music, but she showed little interest. If it wasn't Haydn or Handel, she reminded me, it wasn't really music, and in an instant we were back to the score.

I remembered how the music I played for myself was like the natural extension of my breath; but as I labored under her careful eye, I held my breath for fear that my undisciplined fingers might yield to their natural temptation to go their own way.

Now! . . . too soon. Now! . . . too late. Now! . . . ahh, just right. Now! . . . Oops, too soon again. Painstakingly, I struggled with the incessant beat of the metronome, each click sounding like the unrelenting crack of the whip as it bounced off the walls of the room. Progress was slow.

Time is relative. When I played for myself, the musical stories I explored transformed the hours into minutes. But piano practice slowed time to a crawl. Those minutes felt like hours. Lessons came too quickly and lasted too long.

The energy that had once flowed effortlessly through my fingers was like a river. It bubbled along, finding its own natural course. Left to my own devices, I was content to follow its gentle and sometimes dynamic meandering path. But with lessons, the waters were forced to back up; my body felt heavy with the weight of it, like a dam. It created a tightness and discomfort in those areas of shoulders and back where I had once felt most free. Often, I had played the piano to relieve tension, but now each time I sat with the instruction books laid out before me, I was increasing it.

As time passed, however, a new realization started to penetrate my hardened resistance. I noticed how my fingers strengthened as they adjusted to the new patterns and grooves, ones that were different and more demanding than the usual combination of notes I played for myself.

The chords and note clusters in my lesson books required my hands to stretch in new positions. I learned to be more systematic in my thinking about fingering. I also discovered that the steady practice of scales was introducing a new facility and discipline in my spontaneous playing. As I found more flexibility in my fingers, I became capable of introducing a new dimension of subtlety and boldness into my music.

During the years before I started piano lessons, I had been trying to find and hold the natural flow in my music. But now I was discovering something else: The river flows both ways. Disciplined practice, despite its drudgery at the beginning, offers an even greater freedom later on. My painful efforts to focus my attention on each note in turn broadened my capacity for concentration and enabled me to commit even more hours to practice without tiring. I was also soon to learn that a life freely lived takes no wrong turns. Events have an wonderfully elegant manner of unfolding that is beyond anything that I could strategically plan. Despite my protests in that moment, a foundation was being set for future events that I could not foresee.

Several months after starting piano lessons, the dragon appeared in another form. Every town has its group of street toughs who hang around the edges of the schoolyard. Mine was no exception. Late one cold November afternoon, I walked toward a group of them as I left the school grounds to go for my Tuesday piano lesson. I was about to pass, when one of them looked over and noticed the collection of music books tucked tightly under my left arm.

"Hey, what are those?" he asked. I felt the challenge in his voice.

"Music books," I replied nonchalantly.

"For what?" someone else asked. They all turned to face me now. The one who started took a long last drag from his cigarette and then ground it slowly into the earth with the heel of his boot.

"My music lesson," I replied more carefully. I was annoyed that my voice carried a little less authority than it had before.

They looked at each other and laughed. One of the others stepped forward toward me. "What d' you play?" he asked. Then he stepped closer and blew a thick coil of cigarette smoke toward my face. The air was very still. The smoke circled around my eyes before it broke apart and slowly dispersed in ever-expanding circles above my head.

"The piano," I replied.

"Piano lessons," he mimicked. As he said this, I noticed the hard scowl forming across his forehead. I might as well have said I was studying ballet, or sewing, or even flower arranging, or Japanese brush painting for that matter. It would all have been the same to them.

Just then, a teacher walked toward us. They stepped back to let him pass. I took this opportunity to walk on, too. But just before I was out of earshot, I heard one of them say, his voice dark and menacing, "We'll see you later, piano man."

Their sudden presence that afternoon was a stark reminder of how much my hours at the piano had drawn me into a more aesthetic appreciation of the world. Two weeks before, I had walked far out in the fields near town and watched in awe as a pheasant burst high from a thicket, into the air and disappeared from view. I remembered with pleasure the thick fragrance of the pink blossoms from the cherry tree in the spring. But I also realized how fragile these pleasurable elements could be. Given the choice, any one of these boys would probably have shot the pheasant and cut down the tree.

The following Tuesday was the night of the first winter storm. The music teacher's house was set far back from the street. To reach it, I had to walk up a long, winding driveway past thick shrubs and trees. When I left her place an hour later, it was still snowing hard. Stumbling in the deep drifts, I tucked my head deep inside the collar of my coat to stay warm.

That was probably why the first snowball that struck hard against my leg stung so badly. I had no idea it was coming. It was followed quickly by two more. One hit me on the shoulder, the other on the side of the collar. I tried to run for the street, but the deep snow slowed my progress. More snowballs whistled over my head. Finally, I reached the streetlight and turned to look down the lane. No one was in sight, but from behind one of the bushes, I heard the familiar voice from the schoolyard.

"See you next week, piano man," he said. They laughed, and more snowballs were lobbed my way. Although they fell far short, that did not alleviate the deep pain I felt inside.

Each week now, several boys gathered near the house and chased me home after my lesson. As time passed, some of my friends dropped away, fearful that they too would become objects of the gang's torment. Then one night in late January, I noticed an even larger group than usual gathered among the trees. My lessons were becoming a community event, providing a source of attraction and pleasure for everyone but me.

"I'm taking another route home tonight," I said to my teacher. And, before she could stop me, I had slipped quickly down the hall and out the kitchen door.

Behind her house was a high cliff that dropped far down to the river below. Beside it was another steep incline below which there was a broad ravine. A half-mile walk through the thick trees would bring me to the other side and home. Quickly, I tucked my books under my arm and ran through the shadows to the edge. Before I had any time to think about what I was doing, I slipped over the side. The deep snow broke the worst of my fall. Then I partly slid and tumbled down the steep incline to the trees below.

I lay there for a while. In the distance, I heard muffled cries above me. The gang knew I had left the house, but I hoped they would not try to follow me here. Slowly, I stood up and started to feel my way among the trees. In the silence, I heard the almost imperceptible sound of snow as it settled onto the ground around me. It was a beautiful, delicate sound, soft, gentle, peaceful, and reassuring. In this newfound stillness, nature warmly received and wrapped me in her cloak, holding me close and helping the feelings of isolation and fear dissolve. The shadows around me seemed friendly, like protectors of the dark. For a time, I was content to rest here. It seemed much later when I finally walked the rest of the way home.

It was shortly after that night that I received a collection of Elvis Presley songs. I realized that the piano lessons had given me another unexpected gift: I could read music. For weeks, I explored the songbook page by page. Soon I was able to play the music from memory. I played ballads like "Love Me Tender," and rocked along with "Heartbreak Hotel" and "King Creole."

Spring finally arrived. The snow, now too hard and dirty to form snowballs, melted into the mud beside the streets. As the playing field dried on the schoolyard, the gang soon lost interest in me and returned to baseball and soccer.

One Friday evening, a party was organized at a private home to celebrate the end of the school year. Many students were there, including several members of the gang that had tormented me through the winter months. I saw them grouped together as I came up the front walk. I was just about to turn and leave when one of them spotted me and shouted, "Hey, piano man!"

Then two of them ran down the walk and took hold of my arms. "There's a piano inside; we want to hear you play it."

I had not played in front of anyone but a few friends and family. I felt nervous and scared as they led me toward the piano bench. But there was no place to go. A crowd had quickly formed around me.

It was probably Bach or Handel that they expected, but what they heard was "King Creole" instead. As soon as I hit the notes, I felt the old, familiar rush. My body felt warm and full. This was right. All of the months of practice had helped. There was a strength and confidence in my fingers that had not been there before. To bring inspiration to my playing, the animals, the ones that had been my friends in childhood, joined me as well. To further celebrate this reunion, they had brought along a special guest—the dragon. But he was not dressed in any of the forms that I remembered, particularly the ones that had filled me with fear and weighed me down. Instead, this was the Chinese dragon; his clothes were of vibrant color, and he emerged from the deep waters, beating his belly and breathing fire from his mouth and chest.

Rilke reminds us of those ancient myths in which dragons are, at the last moment, transformed into princesses. "Perhaps," he suggests, "all the dragons in our lives are princesses who are waiting to see us act just once with beauty and courage. Perhaps," he adds, "everything that frightens us is, in its deepest essence, something helpless that wants our love."

How many of us have a story, real or imagined, of a bully taking a carefully guarded book of poems from our hand and reading them aloud to an insolent and indifferent crowd? Who awaits us at the edge of the curb as we leave the safety of the schoolyard and step into the world? If the world around us is, in fact, a reflection of us, is it possible that the person who awaits us is another part of ourselves?

The natural instinctive and creative part of our nature, the one that seeks dignity and love in life, that waits patiently for the world to become a place of love, seems destined to meet many bullies on the corner, including that conforming part of ourselves that would rather be ruled by fear than let this love be seen.

Is it possible that the fear that torments us the most is acknowledging the part of ourselves that wants to receive love? What is our relationship with fear? What is our relationship with love? How much space does each take in our life? Is it also possible that those broken and bent places where fear may find its home are also the places where our deepest capacities for love are to be found? If we dedicate our life to filling this space in a beautiful way, according to whatever beauty means to us, will we also find the place where love and fear can both be respectfully held?

The following Tuesday, I walked again across the schoolyard.

As always, my music books were tucked close under my arm. Several of the older boys were huddled together by the curb, smoking and laughing as they usually did. They looked over at me. I groaned. Not again, I thought to myself. But something was different this time. Instead of blocking my way as they had before, they began to walk alongside. Together we went up the street and turned down the drive, past the shrubs and trees that had concealed them so well a few months before.

The metal fittings from their leather jackets jingled in the warm spring breeze. Their boots, muddied now from the rains, kicked up loose gravel as one stepped up on the porch to knock on the door. There wouldn't be any trouble now, they seemed to say.

They just wanted to be sure that I got to my lesson on time.

Music of
the Spheres

Although our gifts often act mysteriously, they set us on our road early. They do so by using events, dreams, and experiences to attract our attention and map the way. When we yield to them, we are often given a glimpse of another world, one in which colors seem more vivid, sensations more rich, and feelings of wonder and joy more full—all for reasons that are hard to explain. We are touched. Time stands still. For a moment, we sense there is something more, something greater than the cares and concerns of day-to-day life.

Often, the experiences in childhood that evoke these responses are very simple ones, like a game or an activity of some kind. But what may seem insignificant at the time may be found later to be the acorn that grows into the tree. I recall summers close to a large lake; of waves pounding the shore; of the smell of cedar, birch, and sweetgrass; and the image of a music teacher playing a harp, her arms moving in harmony with the swirls and eddies of water as they washed on the beach.

But the image that is most deeply imprinted on my mind came in the form of a dream. It occurred at a time when I lived near Niagara Falls. During that time, I used to go to town each Saturday morning for piano lessons. Sometimes after the lesson, I would walk to the falls and stand near the observation point, just where I could feel the waters rushing over the rocky ledge and tumbling hundreds of feet down into the turbulent basin below. I loved to feel the sensation of cold mist dampening my face. And I loved to hear the thunderous roar of water beneath me. It felt as though the rock and concrete around me were vibrating underfoot.

In the beginning of the dream, I am floating alone in a small rowboat about two or three miles above the falls. I drift helplessly downriver in the fast current. I have no oars with which to steer the boat, and it is leaking. Soon I see the mist ahead and hear the deafening roar of the falls. Then the boat drops into the rapids, where it is tossed violently from side to side.

Within moments, I am swept over the edge. Then there is just blackness. A few moments later, I find myself lying faceup on a raft, floating gently in an eddy just downstream from the falls. I feel surprised and immensely grateful to still be alive. No one, to my knowledge, had ever survived a drop of such magnitude. The sun overhead warms me. I feel peaceful and calm. But just as I begin to enjoy the rhythmic, gentle rocking of the raft, I remember that there are rapids farther downstream. Soon the current starts carrying me in that direction. I am not out of trouble yet.

Just as this realization occurs, I feel myself being lifted gently from the raft and into the air. It happens so gradually that I am not sure it is really happening at all. But soon I seem to be drifting upward several thousand feet above the falls. I feel surprised that I am so relaxed, because I have no idea what is carrying me aloft. Then my attention is drawn even farther upward, to a cluster of large, billowing clouds which form a great circle that conceals the sun. Behind the clouds, long multicolored beams, which originate from the sun's brilliant light, radiate in all directions. Slowly, I drift toward them. As I come closer, the clouds take on the form of a giant cathedral, brimming with golden and yellow light. Music, songs and voices more beautiful than anything I have ever heard before, pours forth and fills the sky.

Then I woke up. Immediately, I tried to go back to sleep, to re-enter the dream, to hear again the richness of the music; but no matter how hard I tried, it was gone. I have had many vivid dreams over the years, some of which I have recorded, but this is the only one I remember in which all of the details are as clear now as they were then.

For the next few hours, I moved delicately around the house, fearful that in some way I might disturb the fragile state I was in. But it was also hard to contain my excitement. I had to tell someone what I had experienced. The first opportunity came a few hours later as I stood shivering in the cold with some of my classmates, waiting for the old yellow bus that would transport us to school.

"Sounds pretty hokey to me," said Timmy, after I had described it to him.

Davey was no more sympathetic. "I bet it's the kind of dream someone has before they *die*." He looked at me with sincere concern. "You'd better be careful, Mike," he said.

Finally, the school bus arrived. I was relieved to be off the hook. The sharing of this dream, which I had thought might be a revelation, had turned out to be anything but. Yet I could not clear it from my mind. Finally, I decided that if I could not speak of it in a way that someone might appreciate or understand, I could play it.

But how? All I could bring to the piano was the question and the hope that the answer might come. But it was hard to avoid the impulse to rush ahead and try to get it done. Often, questions of great power work this way—they have no answers. In the search, we learn that the shortest way to a solution inevitably involves going the long way around. Despite our protests that it is all a waste of time, this long journey is the only way we can create a place within ourselves to which the answers may come. For the larger questions ask us to rest in the unknown, to remain open to the moment and create the space to explore the many ways that composition might go.

After my dream, I went over it and over it at the piano, holding whatever I did in a field of appreciation, until a time came—long past when I had any expectation—when the music opened up and played itself for me. I was filled then with gratefulness, knowing that in this moment, I was witnessing one of the many ways that love can flow.

I wonder how the rush to completion has short-circuited our capacity to move in harmony with these deeper cycles of creation, cycles which by their very nature tend to be patient and slow. The years at the piano have shown me that there can be no intellectual or willful solutions to the great questions that have been presented to me there. "How do I get these two hands to play together?" I ask. Months pass, with great effort and little or no progress. "I can't do it," I say over and over, convinced that this is a waste of time. More time passes. "I still can't do it," I insist. More time passes, until one day, distracted by the gently falling snow gathering lightly on the trees outside the window, I feel something different in my hands—they are playing together. Suddenly, I am sitting at the table with the gods. I don't know how I am doing it, but that doesn't matter—I am *doing* it after all.

Another part of me doesn't see much value in cultivating a quality of listening that is not trying to fix or improve something, but rather is content to simply hear what is being played. Yet to do my work, I need to hear all the voices—those that are impatient and forceful as well as those who keep me at the keys—because the quality of tone I seek is not in the piano—it is in me. Whatever is there is also here, so it becomes important to listen to all of the voices, particularly the one that believes that it is not being heard.

What does it mean when that voice says that this is all a waste of time? What does it reveal about my capacity to form a relationship with the parts of myself that feel awkward, unsure, and slow? Have I become so sophisticated and worldly wise that I am no longer willing to surrender to a process that is not fully within my control? Will I continue to resist even though I know that the search I am engaged in has the potential to define the great overarching and enduring themes of my work, ones that can fill the entire span of my life?

These questions are not intended to have answers. Their power is in slowing us down, in teaching us about the universal laws of time, and in opening our hearts to the patience of love. Questions are an invitation to join once again in the endless and enduring cycles of creation, cycles that are always incomplete and unfinished because there is always more to come. Perhaps if, for one moment, our demands for answers were met: I saw the stages I would perform on, or I saw how long it would take to write this book. It would be too much. The future would seem overwhelming; I would not want to go. Our path is revealed to us one step at a time. Instead of answers, we are asked to hold onto the questions in the faith that in some far future time, long past when we think we are ready for it, the answers will come.

"How do we find the great questions?" we may ask. Through cultivating our relationship with beauty, Ralph Waldo Emerson would say, because "Beauty is the pilot for the young soul. . . . Beauty is the form under which the intellect prefers to study the world."

"So how then do we find beauty?" we ask. For me, it has been through honoring the slower parts of myself. There is a beauty in taking time with myself, in caring for the self-conscious and awkward ways in which these inferior parts of myself engage with the world. As I have done this, I have learned that this brings me closer to the feeling part of my nature and, though this is sometimes difficult, it is also where my true pleasure is to be found.

Doing what does not come naturally is a real test of our courage and an invitation for our love. And yet it also offers great rewards, for the inferior parts of our nature are connected to the larger, more universal dimensions of ourselves. So when we wish to dream, this is where the dreaming part of our nature originates.

For example, it took many years to learn how to stretch the two or three seconds of being in the flow of the music into minutes, then hours, and eventually into a way of life. It has been even more difficult to learn how to fit what now comes naturally into a fifty-minute recording tape. Similarly, learning how to work with words, particularly words that hold the same resonance as the music does, has taken many more years. And organizing these words into coherent paragraphs and chapter headings has taken several years more. At each moment, there is the fear that even though this is my work to do, something will come up that is beyond me; I will hit a wall. There is a way out of this. While we can be sure that an inner voice will try to orchestrate the escape from our creativity by saying that it is all a waste of time, the wiser part of our nature will simply carry on. It knows, as Carl Jung did, that the heavenly music we seek to share is to be found in these inferior and undeveloped parts of ourselves. Over time, we learn to hold them with a quality of patience, understanding, and love. Perhaps it is by living close to these inferior, often forgotten parts of ourselves, that we are most safe, because that is where God is most likely to be found.

Although I sometimes lose a sense of what the question is, the feel of it returns to me whenever I remember the dream. It revealed an invisible world beyond my own, one filled with goodness and joy, a place I felt to be my true home. It broke open something inside, connecting me with a deep desire, a longing and a realization that, if I could not go there, I would find a way to establish it here. Although I had no way to speak of this home, I could play it. I could share with the world some small glimpse of what I had seen and heard.

So my music evolved into a tapestry, a canvas that could reflect the many ways that what was out there, was also right here. It can be found in the intensity of a fiery red sunset, of clouds

gently drifting across an open blue sky, of sunlight shimmering liquid gold on open waters, or of a leaf dancing wildly in the wind. It is to be found whenever my eyes rested upon some place of beauty, including the beauty I found when I could freely rest in and appreciate intimate encounters with others and with myself. It has taught me how to listen with my heart and, through cultivating this quality of listening, how to enter into a kind of flowing relationship with life.

So to stay connected with this flow, I remember the dream, and the dream reminds me that despite the years that have passed, my focus remains the same. It is, in a variety of ways, to sing this one song. Yet how do we find our song in a world that believes there is no song to be sung? I believe it is to be found through opening our hearts to whatever it was that captured our imaginations as children. Often, it is something that so occupied our thoughts that we felt foolish talking about it and yet found we could speak of nothing else. What so filled us with curiosity and joy that words could not do justice to it? Most likely it has been forgotten and buried; it was what had to be sacrificed in order for us to fulfill the expectations of others and live in a reasonable adult world.

I shared this thought one day with a young woman who was working as a cashier in her father's record store. Several years later, we met again. "I went home that evening and asked my father what it was I loved to do as a child," she said excitedly to me one night at a reception. "It changed my life. He described how much I loved fabrics, how I dreamed of textures and cloths and colors all day and night, and, as he talked, it all came back. A year later, I returned to school to study fabric design and now I have my own shop."

We each have to become as a child again if we are to find our own "signature in creation." Even on those dry days when the original dream seems distant, when I have forgotten the questions, when there is no dance and the piano keys feel like mud, the child within me still remembers that it is the purpose of our souls to dream. Unless we keep this dream alive, the time may come, as Friedrich Nietzsche once foretold, when, "Man will no longer shoot the arrow of his longing beyond man, and the string of his bow will have forgotten how to whirl!"

Unless we nurture that which wants to be born, "The world may struggle on but it will have lost its soul. Man will no longer remember how to give birth to a dancing star!"

Visitors by the Fire

They saw us before we noticed them. Two men, muscular and dark-skinned, had just cut through the mist in an aluminum Springbok fishing boat. We had set up camp near Flat Rock Falls. I was leaning against a rock, eating my supper, when I noticed their boat drift to shore. Then the one in front hoisted himself over the bow and pulled it onto the beach.

I was uneasy. Quickly, I looked over to where the other campers were spread out around the campsite. But they were all too busy shoveling food into their mouths, their faces almost in their plates, to notice our visitors. They were also probably too exhausted and hungry to care. The day had been spent paddling and portaging up river against five miles of fast water. Our ankles were sore, and our skin was lacerated with cuts and insect bites and burned by the sun.

We were all city kids, attending our first year at a boys' camp on the northeast tip of Beausoleil Island in Georgian Bay, Canada. We were there to have some fun, play a few games, and catch some big fish. Perhaps we would master a swimming stroke or two. The rocks and water and winds, and rain were simply a back-drop to our plans.

Most of us had not been out of the city before. The names around us—Giant's Tomb, Go Home Lake, The Muskoka, The Moon, and Minnicognashene—seemed a bit ominous. Some were names from Canada's first nations, we were told. Hurons had at one time lived on this shore. Jesuit priests from France had lived among them, and voyageurs had passed by here with their canoes filled with furs. Among these islands and rocks and on the nearby shores, three great cultures had met, and not far from here had been the site of infamous Indian wars. Legends had it that an old Indian chief named Kitchikewana had created this intricate web of islands by throwing great chunks of granite high in the air and watching them land. This inland lake had been formed by a splash from one of Kitchikewana's rocks.

This was our first night away from camp. We had just begun a seven-day canoe trip, and the campsite we picked was just beside Flat Rock Falls, at the northwest edge of a large, unihabited lake. At least I had been led to believe that it was uninhabited until I looked up from my supper and saw these two strange men.

"Hey!" one of our visitors called out as he and his partner stepped into the campsite. By now, the other campers had jumped up, alarmed. We had never seen Canadian natives before. Their presence on this land, however, had been the subject of many stories back at camp at night. Dave, our guide, laughed at our nervousness and stood to shake their hands. He had been on the lake before and knew them by sight.

"Nice night, eh?" the one with the red cap said as he sat on the log by the cookfire.

"Yes," we answered in unison.

"You staying here or going upriver some more?" his companion asked.

"Bala," we said, our heads bursting with questions that we were afraid to ask.

"Bala," they replied. "The water's so low on the river this year you can walk to Bala."

"We almost walked here!" Jimmy said in reply. We all laughed. Jimmy had broken the tension.

"What are you fishing for?" Frank asked.

"Trout, but not much today," they said.

The topic of fishing formed a bond among us. Soon we were learning about the fish, the seasons, and where the best fishing spots were. We knew we were sitting in the presence of masters, adept magicians who conjured up great fish from beneath these waters, warriors who steered their large, powerful boats among the dangerous shoals around the bay. We talked about the big ones that had been caught, muskies usually, or pike, by a man called Corbier. He was larger than life, a legend along the shore.

Amidst the darkening night and the crackling fire, we heard more stories. They talked of the bear that had crossed near their cabin that morning and the moose that were feeding in the marshland at the end of an adjacent bay. They warned of the rattlesnakes that sunned on the rocks across from the falls where we had set up camp. Night fell as we talked, and a cold damp chill settled near the fire, but we were mesmerized. We all hoped our visitors would stay.

Canadian natives had had little relevance to my self-centered and civilized world. But their presence reminded me of a time before school, when picture books of their life, on the plains and by the great lakes, had stirred something deep and old within me. I had mastered the art of the bow and arrow and studied their dress, language, and rituals. Chopin had been one of my heroes during that time, but Geronimo was another; his was among the images of the other great Indian chiefs whose pictures lined my bedroom wall.

Now it was apparent that where their stories of bears and snakes evoked feelings of danger and fear in us, they saw wisdom. This land that was so vast and mysterious and overwhelming in its magnitude frightened me, but it was their domain. Anywhere among these lakes and forests and beneath the stars could be called home. Their connection to it was as wide as mine was narrow. I could recite from memory the facts about a tree, but their knowledge carried the weight and authority of generations behind it. And the animals that we took indiscriminately as resources represented wisdom teachers to them. We lived in different stories, but I had a sense that there may have been a time when the two did coexist. Sitting here watching the embers lift high into the night sky and sharing conversation, I sensed that beyond our differences there was a common bond—something inexplicable and unreachable, a potential, a mystery, a sense of something sacred that was being shared.

Red Cap stood up and stretched. Then he looked over toward the water that rushed over the rocks nearby.

"We don't stay at Flat Rock," he said, his voice conveying a sense of sadness and regret.

"Why?" we wondered aloud.

"A young girl drowned in the falls one day. There are bad spirits here now; no one will stay overnight at the falls."

Then they walked down to their boat. We stumbled behind, trying to shine our flashlights on the path to show them the way. But they were too quick and sure-footed for us. In moments, their boat was launched, and with one tug of the motor, they had turned toward the lake and with a quick wave they were soon out of sight.

I lingered for a moment to follow where they had been swallowed up by the night, but mosquitoes soon chased me back to the tent. Aside from our newfound friends, there was no one in this part of the world but us. It was black and still now. Only the sound of gently rushing water filled the air. And in this darkness, the sounds of the wilderness slowly came to life. A sharp cry of a loon echoed across the lake; it was answered by another far away. Their voices were like an ancient chorus, one that had resonated around these waters from the beginning of time. The soft wail of an owl sounded in the forest behind, and I heard wolves yelping at the end of the lake.

The city was designed for humans; it was there to meet our needs. But here in the midst of mile upon mile of rock, water, and bush, we were only visitors, guests in a land where everything seemed alive but also indifferent to us. Nothing was extraneous here; everything belonged and lived in relation to everything else. Except us, perhaps. Where did we fit in?

Then I thought about how our neighborhood in the city had changed. The wood lot where we loved to play after school had been cleared one day. And the pond where I had watched the tadpoles swim had been drained. As each new day passed, it

II. FRENCH RIVER – OCT 1987   F. HAGAN –

seemed that the world around me was becoming less than I had remembered it. How could I stop this? I wondered. When I played the piano beside the large, screened windows in the camp lodge, I played not only for myself but for the memory of the lakes and the ponds and the trees. I wanted the world to retain its mystery. I wanted the woods to be big and wild enough to get lost in. I wanted the creeks to run deep and dangerous. I wanted the world to retain its sense of anticipation and discovery. I was convinced that it was in the lakes and trees that the music lived. When they died, the music died as well.

Just before drifting off to sleep, I looked out to where a sliver of moonlight had settled between the tall pines and felt, for a moment, a sadness in the gust of wind that rustled the tent flaps.

Perhaps, I thought, there had been a time when humans moved in harmony with the animals, when all of their needs were abundantly met in the wilderness, when the fire was a meeting place for song and story. Perhaps there was a time when the world had not been stripped of its resources but turned radiant in the sun, like a great temple beneath the sky.

For six days we traveled on the river. I learned to dive naked into the cold, rushing water and slug heavy packs for hours over the rough rocks and swamp. I learned to hold the bow of the canoe steady against the forces of the rapids and to listen alert to every nuance in the forest at night.

Throughout all of this, I formed a new relationship with my body, the one that I dragged around during the day and that used to get sick a lot. It knew where to place my feet in the forest at night and how to guide the canoe across rough and windy waters. While my head struggled to find its place in the wildness of this land, my body was responding as if this had always been home. The natural world became my muse. She didn't tell me anything. Instead, she would simply take my hand and show me things. "Over here," she would say. "Look at this bird," or "Feel the bark of this tree."

At first glance, my mind had been intolerant of the apparent chaos and disorder around me, the scenes of buggy swamps and gnarled trees. But as Heraclitus says, "Nature loves to hide." This world asked for my appreciation more than my understanding. As my senses adjusted to these new surroundings, they came to life for me so vividly that I often had to reach out and touch it to just to be sure it was real. The whisper of wind in the pines, the sound of stormy waves lashing the rocky shore, the plaintive chorus of loons echoing through the night, the heat of the sun on granite baking my feet—all of this was like a sonata to my ears.

"Stop for a moment," I found myself saying. "You must hear this. There is a story here and it must be told." The story still lived deep in the hearts and minds of the people who had always inhabited this land. D. H. Lawrence once wrote that "in the dust where we have buried the silent races . . . we have buried so much of the delicate magic of life. In burying these ancient peoples we have also buried a precious part of ourselves." The magic of their stories was in the weave of wind and water, of rock and sun and pine; it ignited my imagination. And just as it ignited my imaginative powers, it also awakened my capacity for love.

I had found my place here. The creativity that lives in me lives here as well. There is a part of me that has never been separate from nature. That part would have gladly placed a piano on one of the windy out-islands of this remote shore and just played for the world.

I have often wondered what it was during those summers that held me in its grasp. Perhaps it is simply that by stepping outside of my familiar boundaries of perception, something shifted inside. It was as if something precious had retreated into these trees and waters, something that could not be accommodated in the city. As I noticed its presence, I felt myself being initiated, drawn deeper into another dimension of life, one that could be spoken of through music but which was more than words. Later, when I looked again upon even the most familiar of sights, I saw something more there. I feel it still when I enter a large northern lake that sits empty of visitors most of the year. I feel a familiar chill in its immense silence at night and the promise it holds that perhaps the gods are near.

Quickly, we guided our canoes down the swift, running water. Skillfully, we eased them through the white water that we had labored up just a few days before. Soon we had returned to the easternmost edge of the bay. We paddled past the islands and through the channels that led us to the open water beyond. The wind was brisk now, blowing up great swells that tossed themselves against the rocks nearby. The wind refreshed and cooled us. The waves caught our bows, throwing spray across the gunnels and rocking our frail canoes like a leaf. We turned them south now into the sun. As we felt the wind push us from behind, we pulled broad sheets from our packs and held them aloft. They unfurled and snapped in the breeze. Within moments, we were skimming along the top of the waves. The wind quickly filled out our makeshift sails and carried us home.

The Quinte Hotel

People often ask what it is that inspires my music. I think of wind-swept waters and vast rolling hills. Or I think about my years as a church organist in the middle of a hushed cathedral, where I could listen to the sounds echo from the high rafters. But I also think about how my music has been shaped and molded through my intimate connections with the human community. And when my thoughts turn in this direction, I think of the Quinte Hotel.

It started one morning when I reported to work with a road construction crew. I had just returned to the city from college, and a relative had thoughtfully arranged this job for the summer. Arriving at 7 A.M., I was informed by the project engineer that I was his assistant. Then he handed me a shiny new hard hat and a clipboard.

Heavy machinery and trucks threw dust around our heads as I helped him survey the roadbed. Later, he invited me to join him for a trip downtown to check for a source of new fill.

"How do you like the engineering program?" he asked.

"It's very good from what I hear," I replied. "I have several friends who are in it." He slowed the truck and examined me closely.

"Aren't *you* in the engineering program?" he asked.

"No," I said proudly. "I am a pianist. I am majoring in music at university."

"I'll be damned," he swore under his breath as he turned the truck around sharply. Soon we were back on the construction site. My shiny white hard hat was soon replaced with a dirty, beat-up yellow one, and the clipboard was replaced with a shovel.

There had been a misunderstanding, and his real assistant arrived later in the week. I was a laborer now, and a few weeks later, I was transferred to another project near a small community a hundred miles east of the city.

Although I liked the new location, I was now far from home and missed the piano that I played in the evenings. I hoped to find another. Several nights later, I found one. It was sitting alone and unused on a small stage in the front of a long, narrow draft room in a local hotel. I had joined several other men from the job site for dinner and a few beers that evening. As we waited for our order, I stepped up on the stage and tried a few keys. The piano was an old, cranky, upright grand. Its keys and strings were grimy from years of misuse. But every piano has a sweetness in it some-where, if I'm willing to take the time with it. The room was empty except for our small group, so I played it for a while.

"Do you want a job?" A stout man stood at the edge of the stage, chewing on his unlit cigar stub. He watched me carefully, waiting for an answer.

"I already have one," I replied.

"Nights," he said. "I just need someone to play from Monday

through Thursday. I've got a fiddler in here on the weekends."

"Sure," I said. "When do I start?"

"Tomorrow." He turned and kept talking as he walked into a small adjacent room. "Come back to my office for a minute." He sat back in his chair. "You're a college boy," he said. "We don't get many around here."

"I'm working with a construction crew out near the air base. I return to college in September. I'm studying at the conservatory there."

"Okay. It's the summer that's busy. I'll pay you a dollar an hour and all the beer you can drink. If you play well, you'll get good tips. Just keep the room happy, that's all I ask."

I nodded. I didn't really understand what he meant about keeping the room happy, but I was pleased to have a piano to play for a few months. The next night, I returned to the hotel, excited to begin my new job.

The room filled quickly. Soon the air was thick with the smell of beer and smoke. Loud, noisy voices drowned out my quiet and thoughtful improvisations. "What am I *doing* here?" I asked myself as the waiters rushed by, their trays heavy with glasses filled to the brim with cold draft. Soon I put aside the ideas of playing show tunes. I left out Chopin and Debussy as well.

On the third night, I found myself absorbed in an arrangement of "Summertime." I moved slowly and languidly through a progression of dark minor chords. The room seemed miles away; I was totally lost in myself. Suddenly, a glass of beer smashed against the wall near the piano. It was followed immediately by another. Within moments the entire room was a brawling mass of bodies. I jumped up and closed the piano lid, stepped off the stage, and walked quickly to the offices in the back of the hotel. There I met the owner, who took me firmly by the arm.

"I'm paying you to keep this room happy. When the room is happy, *this* does not happen. Now go back in there and play something lively. Maybe that will quiet them down."

As he shouted in my ear, several waiters rushed by and threw themselves into the crowd, separating the main troublemakers and regrouping the tables and chairs.

Within moments, I was back at the piano. I started with "Wildwood Flower" and "Rambling Rose," songs that I didn't know that I knew. Soon people were back at their tables, but I didn't stop when they did. That night, I played on and on as if my life depended on it. The small stage felt like an ark in a stormy sea. It was long past midnight before I stepped away from the bench.

I was a different piano player after that night. I no longer got lost in the music. Instead, I learned to feel the *room*. I developed an instinct for letting the music rise and fall according to the moods and feelings around me. As I allowed myself to connect with the room, it gave itself back to me. Soon the anonymous and chaotic surroundings of the Quinte Hotel took on an intimate and human face.

I remember Eddy, deep lines etching his forehead like an old shoe. He watched me for a long time. Then one night, he came up on stage with his fiddle and harmonica. He hummed a tune. It was from World War I, he told me later. Then we played it together. As we did so, tears rolled slowly down his cheek and into the stubble around his chin.

I also remember Mitch, elegant in her long black dress. "Play 'Misty' for me," she would whisper in my ear. But it didn't matter how quietly Mitch whispered. When she left her table and stepped up on the stage, time, and the room, stood still.

There were no more fights in the Quinte that summer. As the days lengthened into weeks, I remembered that the music involved

more than simply getting the notes right. Years of classical training had given me the discipline and focus to perform and com-
pete. But the patrons of the Quinte invited me to explore another
direction. They touched me with their lives. And they taught me
that to connect with the room, I needed to connect with myself
first.

I did return to the music department of the university in September. This setting was so dramatically different from where I
had been, for a while I believed that the summer at the Quinte
had been a dream.

I had almost forgotten the Quinte when, months later, I was
performing a Chopin nocturne for a master class at the conservatory. As I successfully executed a double trill, I accidentally slipped
off the adjacent black key. It was a "slip key" technique that I had
mastered when playing Floyd Cramer's music at the hotel. While
it seemed to fit quite naturally there, it clearly did not belong
here. The students knew this, and so did I. Even Beethoven, whose
porcelain bust stood austerely on a stand nearby, seemed to gaze
at me with a certain displeasure.

"Where did *that* come from?" my teacher asked before I could
play any further.

"Oh that, it's just something I picked up over the summer," I
tried to reply casually.

"Start again at the bottom of page two," he said. "We will talk
more about this later."

We did talk later. He reminded me that further study would
involve a singular and long-term commitment. There would be
room for nothing else. It was time to choose. I thought of the long
years of practice ahead and wondered whether the love I had for
the music could survive the work I would be called upon to do. I
also remembered the Quinte, the meandering nights of music and

conversation, the stories and feelings we had shared, and the lives the music had touched.

It was time to let go of the rigorous demands of classical studies. Though my progress here might be clear, the music that came to me more naturally, from the inside, needed a certain atmosphere of ambiguity to survive. This path inward was not to be found on the written score. Instead, it was time to wander, to drop my focus and be free, for a time, from instruction or advice. I wanted to create a space where I could farm my own soul.

The summer at the Quinte, I realized, was no random accident. It was an integral part of my unfolding life story. As I shared my music with the patrons at the Quinte, they had shared their lives with me. In doing so, they reminded me that although my artistic spirit may try to thrive in the rare, lofty, and virtuous heights and disciplines of the conservatory, my musical soul is really nourished more by going down into the ordinary day-to-day intimacies of relationships and involvements with life. It could not be a monologue performed in isolation. Instead, it was by participating directly in the sometimes chaotic and unpredictable smoke-filled rooms of the Quinte Hotel that I was able to reclaim my own life, and there was more life to be found in one night at the Quinte than in three months in a college dormitory.

When I was younger, I had a tendency to use my art to retreat from the messiness of the world. While I hoped that my work might move others, I also wanted it to offer me free passage, to let me rise above it all and assume a special sitting with other celestial beings who sat together in white robes. But I have learned that we are not so much human beings on a spiritual path as spiritual beings on a human one. We already are what we are striving to become. My work was not to elevate myself above it all, but to uncover this essential part of myself through becoming intimately engaged with the workings of the world.

"Pay attention to this," it says. "The infinite is not to be found out there on some cloud; it is right here, inside this hotel. It is to be found in the sharing of a story that brings tears to my eyes or in the sound of my name whispered on someone's lips. It is felt in those moments of unexpected silence that speak of eternities of unfulfilled dreams. It is heard in the accounts of failure, of setbacks, and of deep loss. Each of these serves as a doorway into a quality of sadness and, through that sadness, into a particular kind of love. The excitement of success can be explained; its rewards are readily understood. Success is also a sure thing—it is complete in itself. But who can understand grief and sadness? These feelings have gravity, they pull us downward, they ground us in the infinite mysteries of the world. It is the moistness around the eyes and the ache in the heart, the lump in the throat and the longing to walk for long hours, to sink our feet into the earth— these feelings bring us not to the mountaintops but into the fertile valleys and perhaps a little closer to home. Success offers us excitement, but failures give us weight, the weight that cracks open the heart to a quality of earthly love that success can never find.

The patrons of the Quinte opened me to this love. They taught me that being really touched by the world involved something more than getting all of the notes right. It required that I alter my incessant focus on goals and achievements, to appreciate that in learning to feel the room, I was also learning to feel myself.

I haven't played in any hotels since the Quinte, but my appreciation for the place and its people hasn't changed. It was underscored recently when I received a letter from a friend who had read a draft of this story.

"I remember the Quinte," he said. "My wife and I booked a room in advance one July day when we were traveling to that part of Ontario from Ohio. We pulled in front just about suppertime. There was a scuffle between several men. Then we saw somebody hit someone else over the head with a beer bottle. We drove on."

That was the Quinte. But life's pearls are sometimes found in unlikely places. It was behind that green and red door, with its grimy, peeling paint, that I first learned to forget myself and discovered what it was like to feel the room.

Wings on the Wind

Carefully, I sat at the keyboard of a large ebony grand piano. It stood prominently in one corner of the dance studio. A stretch bar extended along the far wall. Several early arrivals to the dance class were warming up there. The piano looked elegant where it stood, its glossy finish reflecting off the hardwood floor.

This was a studio and school for modern dance. Although I had been excited at the opportunity to be the accompanist after the interview the week before, it felt strange now. I had not worked with a dance class before, and as more students joined the others to warm up on the floor, I was wondering if my early impulse had misled me. It didn't feel like I belonged here. To relax, I had brought along a selection of sheet music that I could refer to based upon the teacher's requests. It sat discreetly in a box at the side of the piano bench. It offered a little security as I watched the room fill up with dancers and admired how they did their warmup leaps across the floor.

Then Cynthia, the dance instructor, came in. She immediately clapped her hands and gathered the thirty or so dancers into the far corner of the room. "Let's start with an improvisational warm up," she suggested.

"Michael," she said, looking my way for the first time. "Would you play some music with rain in it?"

Rain? I thought to myself. Quickly, I turned to my box and started sorting through the sheet music, looking for something like "Raindrops Keep Falling on My Head," or some other song with rain in the title.

"No, no!" Cynthia said, rolling her eyes and walking quickly across the room to the piano. "Not *sheet* music, Michael, just some notes that have the *feel* of rain in them." Then, sitting down beside me for a minute, she said, "Like this!" She demonstrated by playing a small cluster of notes quickly and lightly in the upper keys.

I placed my fingers where hers had been and began a similar repetitive movement. "Good," she said. Then she jumped up and joined the dancers, who were beginning to explore a movement that felt like rain. Slowly, they stretched their arms high in the air and then dropped them down, letting their fingers flutter lightly toward the floor. This went on for some time, the dancers varying and expanding their movements as the music changed.

I was just beginning to enjoy myself when I heard Cynthia say, "Wind . . . now do wind!" She called out the instructions loudly to be heard above the music.

Wind? I groaned. I was just getting good at rain. And as I tried to get my hands to move from the comfortable motion of rain to do wind, I wondered how often it is that we just begin to get good at one thing when life moves us on to something else. I had become disciplined and skilled in performing the music of Bach and Beethoven, but no one at the conservatory had ever taught me how to play wind or rain. To engage with this work involved drawing upon another form of discipline, one that I had known at one time but with which I had grown out of touch.

Desperately, I looked toward Cynthia. She caught my eye and repeated the instructions again, this time swinging her left arm broadly in a grand sweeping motion. Quickly, my body sensed this movement before my mind caught on. Within moments, my left hand was shaping a complex ostinato movement in the lower notes. Where did *that* come from? a voice inside asked with some concern. But the dancers were moving even more quickly now, and to stay with them I needed to leave my head behind.

"Now be thunder and lightning," Cynthia called out. My fingers tumbled into the bass notes, creating jagged, dissonant chords up and down the keyboard. The images of lightning sharpened my attention. The sound of thunder turned the piano into a drum. I was getting the feel of this now and delighting in the challenge. The dance floor was a whirl of movement. The dancers, despite their numbers, moved quickly among each other without a hint of body contact as they spun around the room.

"Now be like a tree in the wind," Cynthia said. "Feel how it feels as the storm grabs and shakes you."

A tree? How do I create music that feels like a *tree?* For a moment, I lost the flow. Then I remembered the jack pines standing tall and alone on small, isolated, windswept granite islands scattered along the eastern shore of Georgian Bay. I remembered the breezy summer days when I explored these islands with my canoe.

And the push and pull as these great pines were stretched apart by the gusts of the lake's unpredictable winds.

Instinctively, my hands found the notes. The dancers and I explored this experience together. There was no leader and no follower. A shift had occurred here; I was no longer concerned with form or harmony. It was just the energy of the dance that consumed me. I felt exhilarated and free. Just behind me were the scenes on the lake, the rocks, the stormy waters, and the jack pines, standing gaunt and gnarled and bent to the wind.

Then the wind eased, the rain changed into a gentle mist, and the dancers gathered in the center of the circle and sank slowly to the floor. Each note from the piano hovered in the room for a moment, like a fine mist, and then dissolved in the air.

I remembered the days in the camp lodge, sitting at an old upright piano beside a large screen that was open to the juniper, cedar, and rock that stretched across to the open waters just beyond. I remembered the wild winds and dark storms that rumbled across these waters, and the waves that lashed the shore. The rain swept through the open screen, soaking me to the skin. The music was like a soundtrack that unfolded with the changing scenes of the weather around me. As the notes drifted through the screen, I imagined them being picked up and carried aloft like wings on the wind. That's how the inspiration came to me. That's how I imagined I could give it back. Each note was like a seedpod carried lightly across the open waters to some distant island or shore, where it might land and bring forth new life.

How often do we find ourselves living out someone else's dream? "Playing wind and rain is far too simple," they say to us. "You are destined for much, much more." And yet, this original spirit is so easily lost when our plans for it become too large or grandiose. As soon as we bring to our work a sense of effort or strain, or begin stuffing ourselves full of new strategies and ideas, we also lose ourselves and our natural sense of grace and flow.

We are each intended to be masters of something that only we can do. That something often comes so naturally to us that we don't know we are doing it at all. Instead, we code ourselves for struggle. Like that solitary jack pine, we insist on being autonomous and resourceful individualists. We focus our efforts on building our careers, based upon identities constructed on skills and abilities that have often been earned at great sacrifice. Often, acquiring these skills requires great effort on our part, because they are not our primary strengths. The feelings of uneasiness they produce come from an inner knowing, often denied, that whatever this is, it is not really ours to do. Sadly, as we climb the long ladder of success, these natural gifts that originate from within ourselves remain unclaimed.

"Stop for a moment; be still," a small voice says from deep inside. What is that one note that originates from within you that only you can sing? And how can you stay with that one note until it grows into a second, and then a third? What are the images you hold in your heart, the ones in which the notes that most belong to you are held? For me I discovered them again in this dance class. They were to be found in the dynamic elements of nature, heard in the sounds of wind and rain.

The innocence of that one note is often difficult to find and, once found, almost impossible to hold. It appears in one moment of time. Once heard, it cannot be repeated in quite the same way, although the more worldly and clever parts of our minds often try. They recognize its magic and want to use it for their own gain. But this gesture, the one that is free from exaggeration or effect, the one that cannot be contrived, is here for its own sake. It cannot be exploited or recaptured. There is a sadness in realizing that in our very efforts to take hold of it, to make it conform to the way in which we have shaped the rest of our lives, we inadvertently push it farther away.

Recently, a popular singer spoke about how, after the worldwide success of her first recording, she took voice lessons. There was very little budget for the first project, so it was all done on first takes. The follow-up recordings took much longer. Voice training had made her singing much more sophisticated. But it was the naturalness of her untrained voice that had made the first one a hit. As she listened to what she was doing, she realized that she now had the power to impress people with the strength and versatility of her voice, but she was also beginning to sound like everyone else. To hold on to the integrity of her work, she had to keep going back to that original note and let her music organically grow and evolve out of that.

Is there a way of keeping the mystery and wonder of that innocence alive, or does life demand that it be sacrificed as a condition for entering into the world of experience? Once lost, is it possible to bring it back? Can the two coexist? If so, what part does each play in our engagement with the world? Although I have no answers to these questions, I do believe that the universe wants to hear the innocence of that one note from us as much as we want to let it be heard. Perhaps our growing body of experience is intended to labor in the service of just that: to teach us how to preserve the purity of that one note and also guide us in how to share it with the world. We are not alone with our gifts, as we may believe we are with our careers. There are many helpmates around to guide us. If we really want to find our one note for ourselves, all we may need to do is ask and be willing to do the things, however strange they may seem, that will set us on our path. Staying close to this emergent flow is no static thing. It may begin as rain, move into wind, and then empty into something else. The process cannot be reduced to a formula, for it is a living thing.

The light outside the dance studio was fading. The weakening rays of the winter sun reflected off the dust in the air, creating the sensation of a million dancing particles. Ten years of classical training had separated me from this moment and all the early days when I had sat at the piano, searching for my one note, as the waves lapped at the shore. Most of these intervening years had been spent analyzing various musical forms and trying to memorize the score. The dance class enabled me to reconnect once again with the source from which the music I loved could flow.

Bruce Chatwin speaks of the aboriginal creation myths in which, through the practice of singing out the names of each thing that crossed their path, including flowers, birds, rocks, plants, and animals, people learned how to belong to this living world. That afternoon we danced it. And in those moments, as we danced the rain and the wind and learned how to feel a tree, we were blessed in the knowledge that, in the words of Nietzsche, "Nature transformed into love was making its voice heard." Now, in the silence of the early evening, we welcomed it into our midst through the quiet beating of our hearts.

Songs of the Earth

The Ottawa Valley is a unique part of the Canadian landscape. Here, people have added their touch without detracting from nature. Old mills sit by quiet streams, and split-rail and stone fences snake across the rolling countryside. Crumbling old log buildings stand abandoned beside narrow country lanes, their broken panes now empty of glass, their boarded walls mostly concealed by lilac bushes grown wild.

The valley is also a part of the Precambrian shield. Many settlers tried to cultivate this rocky land and failed. The rolling fields are interrupted by coarse deposits of impenetrable granite that have broken many a hoe. The hordes of blackflies that cloud the sky each spring serve as quiet protectors, discouraging all but the most hardy from trying to bend this land to their will.

The shield is gentle and wild, verdant and sparse, vast and intimate. The tall pines rock gently in the summer breeze; the maples stand fiery red and yellow, like lonely sentinels in the autumn cold.

This was a harsh land, dark in many ways, both interior and old. It was a land of struggle and hardship. It moved my soul in ways that I could not explain or understand. Perhaps it was because it was like Wales, a place where many of my ancestors had come from but which I had never seen. I was drawn inexplicably to its roughness, as if among these forested hills and fields gone wild there still existed the remains of an old culture, and within it a mysterious power, one that could make its home only on the edges of the civilized world.

I first discovered the valley when I traveled there from the city to spend time with friends one Christmas. A few days before, I had been offered the use of a friend's apartment to play his concert grand piano and record a tape. The tape was done and, without taking the time to listen to it, I brought it with me to pass along to my friends as a housewarming gift. The morning after I arrived in the valley, my friend John and I were unloading and stacking wood from the back of his truck. It was a cold and crisp midmorning, and snow had been falling steadily since dawn. We worked quietly, enjoying the white, frosty silence in the fields and hills around us. Occasionally, I heard music in the distance. It teased the air but as soon as I stopped to listen for it, it was gone. Then it was back again. Finally, I stopped and looked at John.

"Do you hear piano music?" I asked. I hoped that he would not say no. He looked up, closed his eyes, and listened.

"Yes," he said finally. "It's coming from the house."

I walked over to the house. By now, I was entranced with the music and curious to find out whose it was. As soon as I stuck my head inside the door and asked the question, a voice responded from the back room. "It's you. Haven't you heard yourself before?"

I was stunned into silence. I had been playing the piano for most of my life, but I had not listened to myself before, at least not when I was away from the bench. And the music held an entirely different quality when I was not engaged in creating it but rather simply being with it.

Slowly, I walked back across the yard. I loved hearing the notes drift quietly through the tightly sealed windows and merge with the gently falling snow. Perhaps, I thought, just behind the frantic pulse of our thinking lives, there is this profound sense of peace and stillness in the world.

I returned to the valley that spring and bought some acreage down the road. It had an old barn and the remains of a wilderness Georgian stone house; the blue marble had been quarried from the property many years before. Both the house and barn were surrounded by more than a hundred acres of rolling pasture, marshlands, cedar meadow, and maple bush. Like much of the land in the area, it had been allowed to drift back to its natural state. I loved to wander the land, to be closer to that peacefulness I had felt on that snowy winter morning.

Whenever I walked the fields, I was surrounded by a symphony of sounds—trees greeting the wind, or the intricate array of bird and insect calls. Free from the city, which sometimes numbed my senses and burdened my mind, I could listen to nature's orchestra in a new way. Slowly, I let my attention drift from a leaf, to a rock, to a tree. As I took time to notice things in more detail, I felt myself becoming more intimate with them. When I think of spending hours in these woods and fields, I am reminded of the

poet David Ignatow, who said:

> I should be content
> to look at a mountain
> for what it is
> and not as a comment on my life.

Walking these fields nourished me. In the quiet, I realized how often the problems and concerns in my life became larger than the mountain. There were often days when I walked these fields and heard nothing at all. My preoccupations had become greater than the world around me. But when I was so focused on myself that I became larger than the piano, I could no longer participate with it. I could not hear its sounds and didn't know what it wanted to say. The rhythms of the earth, like those of my heart, are slower than the rhythms of my mind. To let my heart open, it helped to be in a place where I could slow down. I was better able to calm myself when I was in the presence of a larger community, one in which there coexisted many voices and infinite points of view. I was blessed with moments when the trees and grass danced before my eyes.

Perhaps when William Blake said that "there is a moment in each Day that Satan cannot find, one that when it is found renovates every Moment of the Day," he was speaking of simply this. Each moment that I gave to being with a tree was a moment I was also giving to myself. It has been said that the world is a mirror reflection of ourselves. If that is true, and I believe it is, the beauty that I was attracted to here was within me as well. The world changed as I changed, not the other way around. When I created music that was attuned to these sounds, it was not only the notes on the page, but the natural world around me that became my score.

But still something was missing. I wanted to recapture this world the way I had remembered it as a child. There had been an intensity to the world then, to the way in which I heard the buzzing sound of a bee, or saw a path winding into a dark forest, or smelled the fresh mud melting beneath the grainy and coarse spring snow, or anticipated the crash of thunder following a sudden flash of lightning across a blackened western sky on a moist, still night. Each of these experiences filled me with awe. I longed to feel the earth now as I had then. I wanted to be able to say, as Rilke did:

> Oh believe me, you no longer
> need your springtimes to win me over—one of them,
> ah, even one, is already too much for my blood. . . .

But it was a struggle now. The aliveness that had come to me so naturally when I was younger now had to be worked at and nurtured the second time around. It was so easy to let the world become a backdrop to my concerns. As I walked these fields, I remembered the long walks I had taken with my parents on cool spring days. The memories of those walks are as vivid now as the experience of them was then. Perhaps, as children, just a simple walk unalterably changes our relationship with the land, like massaging the part of our brain that was formed during the thousands of years when we spent our lives surveying God's kingdom as we wandered the earth. This might explain Marcel Proust's observation that "the walks of childhood form the raw material of our intelligence."

I felt the absence of this intelligence now, but how was it to be regained? Perhaps it was in relearning how to enter into an experience with something I could not control, to give myself over to a dimension of life that unfolded of its own accord. I could not foresee when the birds would sing or when the clouds would drift across the sky or when the rain would hide the sun. Gradually, I learned to become a witness, an apprentice to my environment. I participated with it in a state of watchful and appreciative silence. The process of creating could not be forced any more than I could force the rain to come or the leaves to fall.

There is a helplessness in this waiting, a frustration, an impatience, like an urgent voice from deep inside, saying, I am important, *make* something happen, I am running out of time. . . . But the fields and sky and woods are indifferent to my concerns. And, as time passes, I find comfort in knowing that the impatience I feel at the piano when ideas are slow to form is not entirely personal. Waiting in watchful silence, not passively but with a pulsating aliveness, is very much the way of the world. It is only through cultivating this quality of attention that we can recognize this guidance when it does appear. It doesn't often present itself in a slow, linear progression like a plodding machine. Instead, it moves in impulses, jumping here and there in leaps and starts. To track it is very much like following the erratic and unpredictable flight of a bird.

When I am able to do this, even for a moment, I have a glimpse, however brief, of a deeper truth. It is a reminder that there is a part of my own life that is spontaneous, natural, and free. It is a part of me over which I have no ownership or control. It has always been there and it always will be. Standing amidst the tall grass swept by the warm summer breezes, I am convinced that the wind swirling around is also the breath of the world. I breathe more deeply, as well. The months that I spent here were an invitation to embark on a new romance, one that involved a pilgrimage of the soul.

This journey was aided by a family of barn swallows that lived in a nest inside the barn, on top of a beam above the dinner table. They had already settled in when I arrived in early summer to renovate the barn. By the time the windows were set to be installed, the young swallows were about to hatch.

I left one window open so the adults could fly in and out to feed their young. I couldn't foresee when they would brush across the top of my head and hover over the table. Slowly, I learned not to duck each time they swooped by, and not to react to their occasional droppings on the floor.

Early one morning, I noticed forty or fifty swallows lined up in a row on the hydro line. Then several swooped low across the field, past the barn, and through the open door of the shed. Quickly, I followed them. There, on the high beams overhead, I saw little balls of grey fluff. I had seen them in the nest early that morning. But I couldn't explain how they had gotten here. Now they tottered and then dropped from the edge of the beam, their feeble wings flapping vigorously as they tried to keep themselves aloft. When one got too close to the ground—and the hungry eyes of the family cat—an adult swallow swooped underneath and scooped them up, bouncing them gently but firmly to the next beam. I was witnessing swallow "flying school." As I watched, I felt a yearning to participate, a desire to add my song to the voice of creation unfolding around me. But to do so I had to find something to play on.

No sooner had I gone in search of an instrument than I found a pump organ, sitting forgotten in the storage shed behind a local church. As I touched the wood and drew the stops in and out, I remembered when I had played an organ like this before. It had been at my grandmother's knee, at an old summer cottage on the edge of Lake Huron, which for me was really an inland sea. I remembered the waves washing high on the shore at night; the pungent, oily smell of kerosene lamps; the rich scent of sweetgrass, cedar, juniper, and pine; the mustiness of moth balls on the sheets; and the insistent whine of mosquitoes against the screens at night. Outside, I imagined strange mysteries unfolding in the blackness of the cedar forest just beyond.

During those evenings, I sat with my grandmother at the organ. As the candlelight flickered against the music books of old American folk songs, she turned and held the pages with one hand, showing me how to push and pull the stops with the other. Then she pressed the pedals to fill the bellows so I would be able to play.

The memory was brief, but it was enough. I bought the organ. One evening several days later, I returned to the church with John, several of his friends, and a pickup truck. Slowly, we loaded the organ in back. Once it was secured, we tried to pack ourselves into the cab again. "Wait!" I said. "It's too crowded up here. I'll sit in back with the organ and play."

It was a long drive home. We stayed off the main highway, using a network of narrow back roads instead. As I sat on the bench, I remembered the swallows, how unconditionally they claimed their place in the world. It was this same free-spirited passion that I brought to my playing that evening, giving myself fully to the organ and letting its sounds soar like the song of a bird.

In this one instant of impulse—the wind blowing against my face, the bouncing of the truck underneath my feet, the sounds of the organ filling the air, the smell of damp earth filling my nostrils—I remembered the world as I had known it. It was to be found in this one moment of engagement, when, like the swallow lifting its young from the ground, I had given myself so freely to the experience that fear had been suspended, and I didn't think to hold anything back.

As the air cooled, a heavy mist settled on the fields and forests. From time to time, we passed a farm set far back from the road. Through the mist, I could see people working in their gardens or enjoying the last few rays of sunlight as dusk settled over the soft, hazy countryside.

And in this pristine pastoral setting, hymns, the ones that I once played with great passion and now remembered in all of their infinite splendor from my years as a church organist, filled the moist evening air. Full, resonant sounds drifted across miles of fields and woodlots and swamp like songs that flowed directly from the earth. I don't know how many people heard the organ that evening, but I'm sure that those who did would have had difficulty locating its source in the misty night air. And I sometimes wonder how many found their way to church the following Sunday, some perhaps for the very first time.

One Summer
in Chimo

The plane trip from Montreal to Fort Chimo on a C-46 used to take six hours. Perhaps now it would be much quicker. But I'm sure that the shortness of the trip would make the entry into this barren and forbidden Arctic setting that much more disorienting.

The first thing I noticed when I stepped from the plane was the blackflies. Clouds of them eagerly hovered around my head, as if I were a lost relative who had just returned after a long absence. The leaden gray sky was so heavy it almost touched the ground. A scattering of people stood around the tarmac; most had on heavy jackets, and almost everyone had their heads protected by finely webbed bug nets. To my left at the edge of the airfield were hundreds of oil drums stacked in rows that stretched almost as far as the eye could see. When I looked over the top of the small, single-story shed that served as the ticket office and waiting room, I noticed another thing: Chimo was perhaps even less than its name. A random smattering of Quonset huts spread out across the small valley. The hills that surrounded it were absolutely naked. Not one was home to a tree.

I was about to step back on the plane, when someone came up behind me and called out my name. Reluctantly, I returned to the tarmac and shook his hand. Others joined him now. They greeted me enthusiastically and asked many questions about what was happening down south. As I talked, they loaded my gear on the back of the truck. Soon we were bouncing along the rough road to town.

"Chimo means friendship in Inuit," I was told. And soon the little community of Fort Chimo, which hugged the west bank of the Kosoak River forty miles south of Ungava Bay in northern Quebec, accepted me into its midst. Chimo had been a refueling stop for aircraft being ferried to Europe during World War II. The original Inuit community was five miles north on the other side of the river. But they had been moved here in the past year so they could be more easily supplied during the summer months.

I was part of a work party that had gathered in Chimo for the summer. The Anglican church and mission house had been moved here from across the river. I had joined as a volunteer to help assemble both buildings before fall. It would be hard work, but we had professional carpenters to guide us and blackflies to keep us occupied if we ever got bored.

During the day I worked high atop the church steeple. I was not comfortable with heights but liked the flies even less—there were so many that I was convinced the area had been designated a sanctuary. But we worked about forty feet above the ground, and very few came that high.

The community seemed devoid of life when I first arrived, but it came together for church service on Sunday morning. I volunteered to play the small pump organ. Many of the more popular hymns had been translated into Inuit from English. Once translated, the hymns took much longer to sing and, if there were six verses to the hymn, they wanted to sing them all. Only one bellows of the organ worked, the second having failed years before. To keep the organ working, I pumped the pedal vigorously with one foot for a few minutes and then alternated to the other.

As I listened to the people sing, I thought about how vulnerable they appeared, so dependent upon this barren land for sustenance and so subject to natural forces over which they had little control. This land gave of its meager resources according to its own timetable, not theirs. And yet I observed, over and over, how their vulnerability was also a source of their strength.

In the culture I came from, knowledge and understanding were paramount, a source of power, one that enabled me to control and feel safe in my surroundings. Vulnerability was considered a weakness. The natural world was seen as an abstraction, something to be examined in a laboratory, not to be seen or experienced firsthand. But for the Inuit, vulnerability enabled them to feel the land, to be intimate with it in ways that I could not explain. They knew things about the land without knowing how they knew.

The Inuit were like heroes to me in one way and yet they were unlike any heroes I had known. My image of the heroic figure was someone who was self-sufficient and aloof, ready to impose his vision on an indifferent and sometimes unseen and hostile world. My hero was set to conquer his adversaries, not seek an accommodation or live in harmony with the land or the objects around him. These people seemed just the opposite, but in ways that are hard to explain. Their actions appeared less head-driven, as though their center of gravity were closer to the ground.

This became apparent one day when a truck loaded with gravel, which a group of Inuit were backing into our construction site, slipped off its makeshift bridge and dropped its rear left tire and axle into the ditch. There it sat, its broad frame awkward and twisted, its grill pointing upward toward a far treeless hill. We were angry—how could the Inuit driver have done such a stupid thing? "These people are like children," we said in frustration, although, having said this, we also felt a little foolish because it wasn't even our truck. But as the community of Inuit gathered around, it was soon apparent that they didn't share our concern. As I spent more time with them, I began to understand why. For them, life was not a haphazard or random series of events, but an ongoing process that unfolded day by day. Every event had a meaning, even though they may not understand it at the time, and therefore they had no fear.

So while we complained that there would be delays and looked around for someone to blame, they looked upon this episode with amusement in their voices and laughter in their eyes. For us, this was just a truck. For them, it was *alive*. This realization shattered any remaining illusions I had that we were a civilized people and that they were primitive or unschooled.

The truck was fixed in a few days. I don't know where they found the parts, but later I learned that there was something almost mystical about how they could fix damaged machinery. According to one person who had watched them repairing airplanes during the war, they astonished officials with the ease with which they put the planes back together, and with how they seemed to view the interrelationships among the parts of a plane as a living system that only had to be healed.

In a moment of insight, I realized that despite the vast differences that existed between their world and mine, there was an attitude that connected us as well. When I sat at the piano and listened closely for feelings of nuance and tone, the inanimate world of strings and wood and pins and steel came to life under my touch, just as their way of relating to the land and to machines brought their surroundings to life for them. It was a sense of connection like a prayerful offering of oneself, a healing, that is effected more through artistry than force. By artistry, I mean a willingness to enter into a relationship with the other, to honor its complexity and aliveness, to engage in a dialogue with it, acknowledging that there is a living soul inside the wood that also wants to speak. Despite their physical strength, the Inuit rarely did anything with brute force. It was this honoring of life that instinctively drew my respect. They engaged their world in a spirit of agility, humor, patience, and appreciation. Their generosity and flexibility taught me a great deal about how to nourish a hospitable place within myself where these same qualities could dwell.

Too often, it seems that we discard humankind's first years on the earth as primitive and insignificant, but the feeling I received in the presence of the Inuit, and in the stories I heard later, suggests something quite different. Recently, I found an Eskimo poem that spoke of that time that they remember so well—the time when animals and humans spoke the same language, when words were like magic and the mind had mysterious powers, when our thoughts had the power to alter our experience of our world. It was a time when a word spoken by chance would suddenly come alive. Nobody could explain it. They would say, "That's the way it was."

After that summer, I could no longer look upon any piano as an adversary that I needed to conquer in order to have my way. The instrument had a power and a soul and a heart of its own; it was a doorway connecting me to a time and place when I and the Inuit experienced the world with a similar magical intensity. And I feel a sadness that perhaps this generation, the one I was with that summer, will be the last to remember this connection, that those who pass away will no longer be replaced by others, that it will be lost to them just as it has long been lost to us.

Through their presence, I also learned that when I was filled by great forces—like fear and joy, feelings that felt too full for words—I could play it all. I learned to trust that the notes could come of themselves, that they existed as living entities: notes that carried not only harmonic definition but also vibration, sound, and rhythm; notes that resonated with meaning; notes that were good enough to be eaten; notes that when they were fully contained within me were also powerful enough to heal. Just beyond the constraints of reason there exists the "art of living sound." When these notes came, they did so unimpeded and unrehearsed and, no matter how valuable they might be, they were gone as soon as their purpose was fulfilled. These notes did not need to be thought through; they flowed naturally from the innate wisdom of what Carl Jung describes as a being that lives within each of us, one that is two million years old. What this historic person has to offer us is a "living treasure of experience and knowledge that can trace its source to the beginning of time." It is something that is given to each of us when we are born.

This is what I found to be so sacred when sitting with the Inuit. In their conversations and stories, these notes were still sounding. For them, they could be heard in the way they spoke. I could feel it in the way in which they formed their words. Words in my culture are rarely held to be sacred in and of themselves. Rather, they are used to win arguments, to convey facts or opinions; often they serve to narrow us down, limiting the ideas and concepts we can hold about ourselves and the world. This living treasure of language, this capacity to let words bring our experience to life, to choose words that are lucid, that serve as clues or signs of what is to come, that are expansive, that invite us to enter into a dance with life—this was an investment that few of us preserve.

"The words we need will come of themselves," Orpingalik, a Netsilik Eskimo once said. Sometimes when they felt themselves to be moved by great forces, the Inuit feared using words. When used too literally, words were found wanting—they could not possibly meet the great groundswell of joy, sorrow, or grief the Inuit were feeling. Then they had to trust that the words would come of themselves.

"When the words we want to use shoot up of themselves," they would say, "we get a new song." It was this musical quality of their words that captivated me. I realized how much nuance and subtle power is conveyed through the spoken word, a power that is often lost when that same word is written down. When they spoke, they didn't only repeat the words, they lived them. They were the words. There was a silent collective "Ahhh" when just the right word was found.

It was this patience and respect that they had with language—the ability to speak directly from their experience rather than speak about it—that grounded their thought in the present and gave power and truthfulness to their words. Sometimes, their voices acted like a tuning fork, inviting another dimension of presence into the room. Then the words were held in a space of profound silence, each word as it was formed suggesting a place that words can point to but where they cannot go.

Is it possible to slow words down? "There are conversations," says Ralph Waldo Emerson, "where we have glimpses of the universe, hints of a power native to our soul." Then the emergent meaning becomes like music to our ears, our words expressing the deep, heartfelt song of the soul. But too often our words are instrumental to something else. To be heard, I feel I must rush along, patching together words as I go, forging a language that is fast, concise, and measurable, fearful that if I slow down, even for a moment, I will have lost it all. I won't be able to make a difference. I will have wasted my life.

Is it possible for us to elevate our own conversations to a level at which the abstractions of our thoughts can be enlivened by the truthfulness and vibrancy of the living word? Can we set aside our insistence upon overrefining our arguments and demonstrating our brilliance in order to walk that fine edge of vulnerability, where we allow the words to form in the speaking of them? And in so doing, can we let the deeper meaning have its way with us and with our place in the world? When I speak from this place, the words and music rise up slowly from deep inside my body and join together in one song. I know when I am near the experience because even when what is being expressed is not emotional or dramatic, I am so touched by the depth of truth in the words that it brings tears to my eyes.

After that summer, I listened to the piano with different ears. Notes were not just notes, nor were they simply devices for worldly gain. Instead, they were a source of truth, a connecting point between the visible and invisible worlds, a place where I could learn to be responsive to its call. I had heard what it meant to truly improvise. It was present each day in the Inuits' relationship with words. The pulse of life that moved them to speak was right here in me too. I didn't need to chase after the notes; they would come to me so long as I was willing to rest in the silence of my heart and wait for them to speak.

As I recall the expressions on the faces of those older men, I wonder how the truth that they once knew can be passed along. What parts of ourselves are holding words that no one else has heard? If we knew that we were being deeply listened to, what is it that we would wish to say? Is it possible for those chatty parts of ourselves, the parts that speak to no one in particular, to rest in the silence, to be content for a time with using no words at all?

As I recalled their darkened images in a dimly lit room, I realized that I had seen their wise and wrinkled expressions somewhere else. My mind struggled to remember where. Then with a shock, I recalled how those same deep, chiseled lines on their faces, the ones that revealed some primordial and mysterious intelligence, are also etched into the face of each newborn child. Is there a similarity in how each holds the world, a shared closeness, perhaps, to something precious, something wise and sacred, something that is not only very old but also very young?

To find it again involves learning how to rest in that childlike, dreaming part of our nature. And though our head may believe that to do this would leave us feeling vulnerable and unsafe in the world, our heart sees no contradiction. It is only through our growing body of experience that we learn how to navigate and manifest our dreams. Our logical mind was never designed to orchestrate this partnership, but our heart is large enough to hold it all. "The mind is not the heart," Robert Frost says:

> I may yet live, as I know others live,
> to wish in vain to let go with the mind—
> Of cares, at night, to sleep; but nothing tells me
> That I need learn to let go with the heart.

Who Will Play Your Music?

Although I spent long periods of time playing my own music, I was uncomfortable performing for others, with the exception of close friends. Instead, I did covers of other people's music and relied upon these arrangements when I played in public.

It was one of these arrangements I was exploring while sitting at a piano in a hotel lobby one quiet evening. I had been at the hotel for several days, leading a management seminar. We had given ourselves the night off. Now, I sat for a time, lost in my musings. The building around me appeared to be so quiet and empty that I even felt free to let some of my own music weave in and out of these musical conversations.

It wasn't *that* empty, however. Soon an old man walked unsteadily out of the nearby lounge and plopped himself into a big easy chair beside the piano. There, he slowly sipped his wine and watched me play. I felt distracted and uneasy, trapped on the bench, where any moment he might request one of his favorite tunes, one I most likely did not know how to play.

"What's that?" he asked when I was done.

"Oh, a little bit of 'Moon River,'" I replied.

"Yeah, I recognized that," he said. "But there was something else before it, what was that?"

"That was some of my own music," I replied. "I don't have a name for it yet."

"You should," he said. "It deserves one." He looked thoughtful for a moment, then he said, "Your music is beautiful, but you're wasting your time with that other stuff."

His comment dropped into my lap so quickly I wasn't sure I fully understood what I'd just heard.

"What do you mean?" I asked.

"It's *your* music that brought me out here."

"But . . ." I said, cutting him off. "It's the other music that people want to hear."

"Not when they hear this," he replied. "Please, play some more." Then he closed his eyes and sat back in his chair.

When I am being deeply heard, playing my music feels less like a performance and more like an intimate act of love. I become more conscious of being carried along by a current of feelings, and following these feelings becomes more important than holding to the accuracy of the notes. Perhaps it is when we are in the company of another, particularly one whose appreciation for our work knows no bounds, that this love is most likely to be found.

When I finished playing, he and I sat together quietly for a long time. Slowly, he opened his eyes and sipped again from his glass.

"What are you doing with your music?" he asked.

"Nothing," I said. "It's just something I do for myself."

"Is that *all?*" he replied, surprised by my words.

Then I explained briefly what had brought me to the hotel.

"But how many others can do this consulting work?" he asked.

"Oh, perhaps twenty or thirty," I said, adding quickly, "but I don't want to give it up; my mission through this work is to change the world."

"I'm sure it is," he said. He seemed unmoved by the forced conviction of my words. Then he set his wineglass down on the table and looked directly at me.

"But who will play your music if you don't do it yourself?"

"It's nothing special," I protested.

"No," he agreed. "But it's you, and the world will be poorer without it."

I was about to offer other excuses when, with fire in his eyes and a voice sober and clear, he said, "This is your gift—don't waste it."

With that, he stood up, steadied himself by resting his hand on my shoulder for a moment, raised his glass in a silent toast, and then weaved slowly back to the lounge.

I sat frozen on the bench. Who will play my music? I asked myself over and over again. An hour or so passed, but I was still in shock. In his memoirs, Chilean poet Pablo Neruda speaks of how people who have lived unfulfilling lives sometimes complain that no one gave them any advice. No one warned them in advance that they were off course. But this was no longer true for me—I had just been warned.

Later, I went in search of this man, to insist that he tell me more. But he was gone, and a part of me suspected that perhaps he had never been there. If I had not heard his advice on the bench that evening, something else might have happened—a dream, perhaps, or an accident—to get my attention. For some people, it is the ending of a relationship or the onset of an unexpected illness—something comes along that brings our lives up short. What we had always thought secure suddenly becomes finite. In that moment, the larger universe, of which we have always been a part but often ignored, has our full attention. Its presence can be as dramatic and frightening as a raging storm at sea or as gentle as the intimate act of kissing the princess awake. It knows how to find the weak point, the undefended part where we are most likely to yield. This one wake-up call is enough to set us on a path. Following this path as it spirals inward and outward, and honoring it, even though the purpose of it and the final result may remain unclear, becomes our new work. "The truth dazzles gradually," as Emily Dickinson says, "or else the world would go blind."

Often, I imagined that my true vocation was to be a painter, or a poet, or something else equally remote or extraordinary. When friends asked about the music, I was emphatic in my reply. "No," I would say. "This is something *special*." But there is no mystery to the work that is ours to do. Although it may appear to be some attribute situated in the heavens somewhere, it is often found in the familiar and ordinary and located close at hand. Indeed, it is the idea that it should be special and extraordinary, that it is something out there—remote, elusive, and difficult to do—that throws us off track.

What is ours to do comes so easily, because from the very beginning it has always been there. It may not necessarily be a special talent like writing or music; it may instead be a quality of caring that we offer, a capacity for listening deeply to others, or simply the wonder and beauty we bring to the world through how we give our attention to a piece of music, a flower, or a tree. Our purpose is to give ourselves to the world around us—including people, musical instruments, trees, and words—and through the attention we bring to them help them blaze to life. When we offer ourselves to the world, the world gives itself back to us. In the words of D. H. Lawrence, "Life rushes in."

What is it that we desire to do that brings an increase to life? This often offers a clue as to where our gifts are to be found. Beneath the long list of things we *must* do is a deeper purpose, one that involves being present with ourselves and, in so doing, bringing some aspect of the world to life. But we cannot do it alone, for the recognition of who we truly are is most often found through the other. "The mystery of creation was always between two," Laurens van der Post writes, "in an awareness that there was always both a 'thou' and an 'I.'" We all need at least one other person to recognize this spark in ourselves, to make us the one we were meant to be. For me, it was that man in the lobby of the hotel.

Who is it that offers the act of confirmation in your life, the one willing to hold the match to light the fire to set your gift to the world ablaze? And who, or what, does your gift serve? As Laurens van der Post says, "most of us indeed have become distorted into knowing only the 'I' of ourselves and not the 'thou.'" Yet, once ignited, the flame that burns within us does so with such intensity that we would go blind if we looked upon ourselves directly. Our "thou" is seen through the actions of others in relation to us; they are the moons that reflect back to us the intensity of our sun.

When I said yes to that moment, I was relearning how to say yes to the pleasure I knew the music would bring. But I was also opening myself to the fulfillment of larger intentions, ones that were not entirely my own. I trembled at the thought. Sometimes others have already tried to set our lives ablaze, and we have not accepted the match. We know that once the genie is out of the bottle, our lives will never be quite the same. There is burning that takes place, burning that has the power to transform to ashes old, limiting beliefs and everything else that we hold to be true. Nothing is exempt; everything may change, including even the smallest of acts.

After that night, I knew I wouldn't be playing anyone else's music again. And when I met the group in the morning, something else had changed as well. We were working on the value of purpose and vision, but I could no longer speak of it with much conviction. I realized that I could not be very helpful to others about purpose until I had done something about fulfilling my own. There was a part of me that had always been a musical soul, but it had often been difficult to rationalize my time at the piano with respect to the achievement of any tangible outcomes or goals. I often felt frustrated and helpless when I saw little progress after a long day of work, and there were few guarantees that my efforts would ever result in any worldly success.

Yet this time, I could not stop. Whatever vision I now created for my life would have little value unless it included the practice of my art. There was a part of me that clearly did not want to let go of what was familiar in my life, but I also knew that the safety I felt was an illusion, for when we turn away from what we love, there is no longer room for magic in our lives; they become narrower and narrower until we meet a dead end. This moment of choice contains within it great potential and great risk. The hands that are there to guide us cannot help us until we step into the unknown. The story we create for ourselves now reveals how we are living the question that physicist Albert Einstein once asked: "Is the universe a friendly place or is it not?"

"I am too old," some might say, or, "I would be lost without that job." Sometimes, we find that our body struggles with itself—one part eager and willing to step forward, another part holding back, acting like a troublesome family that is not all growing and expanding at the same pace. Within my heart lived a wise and musical soul who wanted to merge with the heart of the world. Inside my head presided a middle-aged achieving and educated mind that felt it could do it all on its own. Beneath it all are the legs of a ten-year-old boy who still holds some fear of the world and does not want to venture far from home. My educated and strategic mind, which had played a significant part in masterminding my progress to this point, would be of little help when it came to changing it. "Consulting is your real work," it kept saying. "Why be swayed by the irrational ramblings of some drunken old man?"

Then several weeks later, I met a participant from a previous workshop on a busy downtown street. "That was a great program!" he said to me enthusiastically.

"Really?" I replied, my head feeling inflated now with the sound of his words. "What did you enjoy the most?"

He thought for a moment and then said, "The night you played the piano; everything was great, but *that* was a real surprise."

"The piano," I said. The internal voice was very silent now—my legs felt weak as well.

Then he went on to say, "Look, if you ever do anything with it, like a recording of some kind, let me know."

With that he pressed a business card in my hand, wished me luck, and disappeared into the noon-hour crowds. As I watched him go, my head was swimming but my heart felt very full.

In my hand, I held a promise and a possibility—it was what I had always longed for: the chance to bring into life something that had not been there before, to turn some personal and precious part of myself inside out and, in doing so, to deepen my sense of belonging in the world. Musical ideas, long dormant, filled my head. It was only at the piano keys that I found any rest. There were days when I felt dizzy, as if I were on some high mountain ledge, when in fact I was simply standing beside the kitchen sink. My head was fearful that I was losing control. My body knew that I was coming home. I was inside a contradiction, ignited, on the one hand, with a vision that filled my soul, and on the other, trapped inside a web of limitations that did not trust in the existence of a soul at all. Was it possible for the longing in my heart to hold it all?

I could neither push forward nor go back. When we reach this step in our creative life, we are often asked to go beyond our skills, to do the opposite of what has gone before. If we have been unfocused, it's time to focus; if we have been driven, as I had been from time to time, it's time for space. Nourish the longing, Kabir says to us, for it is the intensity of the longing that does all the work.

Yet we cannot be casual about this step, either. To turn our attention from our longing, even for a moment, may be one moment too long.

Ten years ago . . .
I turned my face for a moment

and it became my life.

These words were written by a participant in a management workshop lead by poet and author David Whyte. How many of us have turned away from living an imaginative life? How many of us would rather sacrifice ourselves to the security of institutional life than engage with the volatility of a soulful one? What is it that so often compels us to turn away from our longing rather than into it? Perhaps the dream seems so distant from the reality we live with day to day that we simply don't know where to begin or how to find a convenient time to start. There is also an awkwardness in our initial attempts to put ourselves into our art. We can feel unsure and self-conscious—quick to judge our progress and ready to admit defeat in the presence of those who say what we are doing is silly or frivolous, or through the constant pesterings of our own self-doubt.

When we take these first tender and delicate steps into our own imaginative life, we often need a bold and fiery image, one large and intense enough to make it a part of ourselves until our own small, gentle fire is strong enough to burn on its own.

It was on one such day, when I didn't know where to begin, that I felt the presence of Beethoven beside me on the bench.

He looks on life to ponder . . . sunk in the lowest depths
of his dream . . . one look has shown him the essence of

the world; he wakes anew and strikes the strings to sound the dance the like of which the world has never heard. It is the whole world dancing: frenzied joy, the cry of pain, the transports of love, the acme of bliss, fury, riot, agony, infatuation, suffering. The lightning flickers and the thunder growls. Leading us masterfully from whirlwind to cataract, to the edge of the abyss . . . and now the night beckons, his day is done.

When I read this account by Richard Wagner of a performance by Beethoven, I realized that I, too, experienced moments when I was intoxicated with the music, "drunk" with abandon, drenched in sound. I was the music. The moment was filled to overflowing. I could hold nothing back.

Could I, like Beethoven, hold a vision large enough to fill the entire span of my life? Could I say yes to it all despite the setbacks and confusion and self-doubt? Could I not only accept but embrace the uncertainty, not only tolerate but engage the ambiguity? Could I step forward and meet the suffering, the bliss, and the frustration? Could I willingly receive the future with a humble and prayerful acceptance and say, as philosopher Rudolph Steiner once said, that "whatever the next hour or day may bring, I cannot change it by fear or anxiety, for it is not yet known"? The terrors I feel may simply be shadow images from a more limiting past, not predictors of times to come.

When I left consulting to begin sitting at the piano again, I believed that I played poorly. And I had little experience with writing when I later took time from music to begin working on this book. Perhaps this is what life asks of us—to step faithfully into that very place in our lives where we can no longer fall back on our cleverness or wits. To serve the impulse to create is to accept that it may ask everything from us and offer little assurance in return. Moses guided his people into the Red Sea on faith; they were apparently up to their necks before the sea finally parted. Perhaps it is only when we have emptied ourselves of all guarantees that life finds us. "Providence sets in," as Johann Wolfgang von Goethe says, and a way opens before us, one that cannot be seen in advance.

The day after meeting the old man in the hotel, I had asked how I might bring my music to the world. After what seemed an eternity, an answer finally came.

"Cassette tapes!" my accountant said to me one afternoon.

"What?" I replied with disbelief.

"Cassette tapes," he said again. "You were asking about how to write off some portion of this new grand piano, and I said make a cassette tape of your music and sell a few."

I recalled the man on the street who asked about tapes, and the friends who brought their tape recorders when they came to visit. The help had been there all along but I had not yet been ready to hear it.

Six months later, I arrived home with the cassette tapes. And after a few weeks, I received a phone call from someone, a stranger, who had heard a tape at a friend's home and wanted to purchase a copy.

This was an important moment. I had been so intoxicated with the excitement of producing my own work that I had forgotten that it was actually going to be heard. For years, I had been taught that the only music of any value was what was notated on the score. But I had released something different, something of my own. In doing so I had broken a bond of quiet conformity. I was no longer immune to the attentions of the world. Suddenly, an impulse overcame me to hold it back, to protect it like a parent wants to protect a child from being hurt. But our gifts are not given to us to be used only for ourselves. They are intended to be shared. Despite my fears, I sent the tape.

In the following months and years, I sent out many more. And as knowledge of my recordings found their way around the world, my identity changed from being a busy business consultant to a wandering troubadour. But this was also a time for reading and thinking and taking long walks. I was responding to another impulse now, one that seemed to contradict the expectation that this was the time to establish my celebrity. It was a desire to be responsive to a deeper need, to take refuge, to create a quiet space in my life in order to find a deeper truth within myself.

"I am not I," Juan Ramón Jiménez says so beautifully in the opening line of his poem, "I am not I":

> I am not I
>   I am this one
> Walking beside me whom I do not see,
> Whom at times I manage to visit,
> And at other times I forget.
> The one who remains silent when I talk,
> The one who forgives, sweet, when I hate,
> The one who takes a walk when I am indoors,
> The one who will remain standing when I die.
>
> (Trans. by Robert Bly)

The encounter with the old man had encouraged my return to music, but it offered something more. Being at the piano had opened a pathway in which I could feel once again the tenderness that lay deep within my heart. And as my heart opened, it, in turn, offered an invitation to a wedding—a marriage between the ambitions of my intellect and the yearning for a deeper truth that was emerging within my soul. I was learning to love the other half of my self.

As I experienced their joining together, I was saddened by the years that had been lost, the times I had willfully struggled to try to get everything right when I didn't know what right was. They were times of planting seeds and then impatiently digging them up to see if they had grown, of trying to figure out what others wanted from me instead of asking what I most wanted for myself, of feeling the fear of not knowing where this was all going to lead, of believing that I needed to rely upon the individualistic and achieving parts of my nature to do all of the work, because I did not believe in asking for help.

Learning to trust that these terrifying leaps of faith are in fact *of* life and not *against* it came slowly for me. And I am grateful now for knowing that perhaps it is when we feel truly lost, groping our way somewhere between the in breath and the out breath, that the gods are most near.

As the years passed, I found myself returning to the consulting work I had done before. But something is different now. I no longer need to fulfill the expectations of others or leave any part of myself at the door. I had thought that the step into music would be the completion of a life's work. But a conversation with a friend a few years ago revealed that perhaps there is now a new chapter forming in what is unfolding as a composition of my life.

He is the founding member of a musical ensemble that has been touring together and doing brilliant work for more than twenty years.

"How have you stayed so fertile and creative for so long?" I asked. We were warming ourselves by the woodstove one cold December day.

He thought about my question for a moment and then replied, "We don't talk." Seeing the shocked expression on my face, he added by way of explanation, "We tried years ago, but our personalities and outlooks are so different that if we had continued to try, we would not have survived very long as a group."

I thought about his comments for a long time. Is it possible that while the arts can help us open the heart of the world, we also need to hear our and others' voices if we are to truly ignite its soul? How often have the complex problems we face remained unsolved because of our incapacity to talk with one another? Is there also an artfulness and wisdom to be found in our capacity for deep and generative conversation that reflects the truth of the words of Henry David Longfellow that, above all else, "the human voice . . . is indeed the organ of the soul"?

How do we discover in words the same depth of truth and inspiration that flows from our hands when we paint or our dancing when our feet touch the floor? Is it possible to suspend our schedules and routines to experiment with the deeper insights that can emerge when we are free to bring our different voices forward without fear of embarrassment or concern? Can we share our most deeply held beliefs with the possibility that behind them lies an even greater truth, one which, once revealed, might allow

us to live in a more imaginative and peaceful world? To help answer these questions, I have returned part-time to the world of
business. When left to its own devices, our intellect can do vio-
lence to ourselves and the world. It needs to know that it can
release its fear, that the creative power of the imagination, which
speaks of the essence of who we are, is always near.

My work has come full circle now. I believe that there is a new
human story to be written, one that speaks not so much about
the accomplishments of great men and women, but another. It is
an exploration into how to balance the achievements of our mental intelligence with another form of knowing, which comes from
the insight and creativity that can find its full expression only in
a group. "The new saints will not be individuals, but communities," a friend observed one day. As we join together, we may be
able to hear behind our own voices, the one voice, the sound that
Longfellow describes as "the flowing of the eternal fountain, invisible to man."

When I set aside my consulting practice to return to music, I
could not foresee where it would lead. But over time, the painful
uncertainties have evolved into a wonderful dance that elegantly
weaves together all of the various significant but seemingly separate strands of my life. Finding the marriage between my intellect
and my soul could not have been planned, at least not by me. It
would have been too complex and perhaps too terrifying for my
strategic mind to grasp. But perhaps, just as Wagner spoke of
Beethoven's spontaneous and deeply felt performances as being
"child's play" for him, creating our lives so that they are a reflection of what we love is child's play for the heart.

So now when I join these groups, I don't bring charts and

theories and projectors as I did before. Instead, I simply bring myself and a nine-foot-six-inch concert grand. And as we form into a circle, I'm careful to save a place beside the piano for the old man from the lobby of the hotel.

Images on the Reel

"What was that?!" I said with alarm as I pulled the headsets from my head.

"Water," Terry said calmly.

"Water?" With the headsets on, it had felt like it was coming right over my head.

"The headsets amplify the sound," Terry explained. "Someone just flushed the toilet upstairs."

I had sat here at the piano for many hours, but I couldn't remember ever hearing the toilet flush before.

"Well," Terry said with resignation as he pulled the first microphone from the stand, "this is a great set, but it does tend to pick up everything in the house. It was picking up your breathing on tape, too, so I knew we'd have to try some others."

He also knew that I was annoyed. This was the sixth set of microphones we had tried. The first had been fine, but the rest had each demonstrated some drawback. Terry was a perfection-ist. He wanted to be sure we had exhausted all possibilities before we were done. I was trying to be patient. I had insisted that I wanted to record my music at home. I was convinced that in a relaxed and natural setting, I would best be able to capture the spirit of the music the way I liked to play it. I had already tried recording in a studio, but I had felt entombed behind tons of concrete, cut off from the images of nature that inspired my work.

Playing my music was often immediate and spontaneous, but trying to record it was becoming anything but. Finding the right microphones was one problem, quieting the house and the neigh-borhood was another. Trucks rumbled down the street and air-craft flew overhead. When it turned too cold outside, the win-dows tended to crack. The refrigerator and furnace had to be turned off; sometimes I forgot to turn them back on. The damper peddle on the piano thumped—we put a large pillow underneath it to make it stop—and the felt dampers would rise and drop onto the piano strings like the raspy breathing of an old man. I finally found a piano technician who was willing to trim the felts with a razor blade. It was difficult and painstaking work. And there was the ongoing concern that perhaps this could not be done, that the living presence that was in the music when I played for friends would simply not be there when I tried to capture it on tape.

But these setbacks and frustrations were nothing when com-pared to the terror I felt several nights before I was to record. I had been so preoccupied with selecting the equipment, prepar-ing the room, listing all the possible sources of noise, that one night I awoke in a state of panic: What am I going to *play?* I thought of the days we had listened to the test recordings. I felt so ex-

posed. There was nothing but the piano; there were no other instruments to cover up the wrong notes. For years, I had been
content to live in the shadow of other people's imagination. When
I began to explore my own, I did it mostly for myself. Nobody
took much notice of my work then, and the music flowed freely
by itself. But it quickly eluded me when others brought their ears
into the room.

"Make friends with the microphones," Terry said to me. But
they made me self-conscious; they were like giant ears of the great
masters, their heads bent over the piano, their noses not six inches
from the strings, critically examining the worthiness of each and
every note. With all of the music that lay behind me, what could I
possibly add? During my years of classical training, I had responded
to the impulse to reshape, delete, add, and, in many other ways,
improve upon their work as much as my own. They were master
improvisors, I would say in my defense. But my teachers were not
interested in my indulgent ramblings; they wanted structure and
form. And it was their voices that I was hearing now.

How am I going to organize it all? I asked myself that night. I
was a musical painter: the keyboard was my canvas; my fingers
were the brush. How was I to transfer these images, often ephemeral and conceived in the moment, onto this revolving reel that
sat beside the bench?

Although I enjoyed the labor of crafting an overall structure
for the music, I also wanted to leave a significant amount to chance,
to keep it loose and free so that it became a weave of thoughts
and questions rather than a completely finished work. When I
could find that edge and hold it, I wasn't so much playing the
music as I was allowing it to unfold. And the music that seemed

most magical, where the notes hovered transparently in the air, was contained in the ideas that appeared as if by accident, not in the compositions that I planned to perform that day. Entering into this dialogue with the piano often evolved slowly. It was a moment of timelessness when everything stood still. But these visitations could not be pushed, nor could they be scheduled in advance.

But the recording tape was unforgiving. By the time I felt the music dance beneath my fingers, the tape that was recording it was almost over. When the dance wasn't there, I often felt off center, uncertain as to what was to come; then it was easy to hit many wrong notes.

Given all the difficulties, there were many days when the music fell short of the vision I held for it. I felt the fear that perhaps grips each of us when we create. The world may never hear the deeply felt song that I am capable of. Those moments of magic might never leave the privacy of this room. I would be unable to set my "love gift" free. Whatever I may do will feel incomplete. Perhaps it is this desire for perfection that stops us in our tracks. Nothing quite measures up. The tyranny of our judgmental mind never allows enough room for the more tender, searching, and developing parts of ourselves to find their way onto the page. The essence of what we hear in our heads may never translate exactly the way we want it. Yet, when I listen closely to what I have done and get past all the ways that it is different from what I want, I also hear something else. Sometimes it is better than the plans I had for it. It's like a scattering of "fairy dust" has touched my work, and I know then that I am not working for myself alone. It is this that brings me back to the piano each day—the possibility of finding this something more, of being surprised by my own work.

But that possibility was forgotten now. That night I was filled with despair. Despite my hopes for it, I felt alone with my work. A fear of disappointment gripped me, an awareness that the inspiration that moved my music was not entirely within me, and therefore could not be reliably predicted or controlled. It had no interest in repeating itself and it would not conform to any formula or plan of approach. It was this unknown that haunted me, not knowing whether I could connect with this inspiration-on-demand and, if I did, how it would show up. I had to catch it on the fly. If I tried to work it all out beforehand and play it exactly as I had before, the wild gypsy spirit that lived for the moment would not be new and fresh. Then, instead of taking flight, the music would feel like some caged bird. The work is a living presence; it cannot be enslaved or stored in a vault. The mystery of creation works this way: We work and plan and break our backs for it. And then, in the ashes of our struggle, it appears like a gentle wind rustling through blades of grass. To find it seems impossible and yet, once here, it is as if it has always been this way.

Finally, our recording day arrived. I greeted Terry at the door. He stood smiling broadly with all his equipment in tow. "I have another pair of microphones to try!" he said with great enthusiasm.

For the first time in weeks, I said then what I should have said before, "Nooo!"

Terry looked at me once and didn't even think about arguing. As he readied his equipment, I reminded him that, regardless of the outcome, *this* was to be our last day. Within a short time, the recorders were set up and we were ready to go. Being open to the flow of the music was not going to be enough for this day. It also had to be fired by the love I held in my heart for what I intended to play. My preparation, I discovered, had not been in simply trying to figure out which notes to play; it had been in learning how to prepare myself for this moment: focusing my attention, deepening the encounter with the artistic part of my nature and listening closely for what it was that it wanted to say.

In the moment I said no to Terry, I was saying no on behalf of all artists to those insistent and demanding voices that try to suggest that our experience is not enough, that others are more qualified, and that perhaps we should consider doing something else. The breadth of the universe is contained inside our experience. It is more than enough. We grow into the work as we do it; the forms and structures unfold over time. In the beginning, it is sufficient for us to simply start, to show up, to let what we do be the embodiment who we are, and, in so doing, to be fully ourselves.

But even within this newfound understanding, I didn't know where to begin. And in that, I discovered something else. Forms and structures and conclusions were essential, but they needed to be held lightly. Whatever I clung to, whether chords or words was useless over time unless it could freely give way to something else. So, as I sat down at the piano bench, I was ready to simply give in. Instead of trying to hold it all together, I emptied my mind of all its ideas of goals and accomplishments. It was time to set everything loose and let it scatter in the wind.

I played for two hours that cold January afternoon. There were no breaks, no repeat takes, no outside noise, and no wrong notes. I'm grateful in knowing that to do just this with the music is enough. It is changing me and perhaps doing its work in the world, even if it never leaves this room.

When it was over, Terry looked at me and finally breathed again—perhaps for the first time that day. Everything was recorded, he reassured me, and everything was okay.

Finding My Own Way

Our creations are not ours to keep. The time comes when we must present them to the world, sometimes before we think we are ready. I could feel it now. The universe awaited, hushed, expectant, filled with anticipation, ready for me to make my move. But no move was forthcoming. Impatient now, the universe could wait no longer. Finally it spoke:

"Where is your tape, Michael?" a friend said one day on the street. "I hear you have the recording done. Now I want to hear it."

"Uhh, soon," I replied a little defensively.

"What's holding it up?" he said, curious upon hearing the hesitation in my voice.

"I don't have a title yet," I finally admitted.

"A title. You mean you're holding this up because you don't know what to call it?"

"Well, it needs something," I tried to explain. "You just can't release something without a name."

"Michael's music," he said.

"What?"

"Michael's music! That's what we all call it. Each time I try to explain your music to someone, I get lost for words, so I just shrug my shoulders and say, 'It's Michael's music.'"

Two months later *Michael's Music* was released. Most record releases involve the preparation of advance press kits and promotional programs for radio and newspaper. Mine involved carrying three heavy boxes of cassette tapes into the basement.

"What am I going to do with all of these?" I moaned to my wife, Judy, as I lifted each box from the car. I eased them carefully down the steep stairs and stacked them along the west wall. Two hundred and fifty tapes was the manufacturer's absolute minimum order. I was sure that all would remain stacked there for months, perhaps years.

"They'll be gone in three months," she assured me, and she was right. In less time than that, they were all given away or sold. It taught me that as we expand, the world around us expands as well, for each step that we take, the universe takes two. The first tapes went to friends and family. Others went out to people who had ordered them in advance. People loved the music, they told me. I glowed with satisfaction. But the universe wants everything from us, and we must be careful that it does not push us too hard. I was still basking in the warmth of my sudden and unexpected success when, all too soon, these same people were asking for more.

This time composing progressed more slowly. When I had prepared the first tape, I had only myself to please. But now I had an *audience,* and I realized how easily some of the initial innocence is lost when others take notice of your work.

"Try more minor notes this time," one suggested.

"No, don't do that," another said. "I use the music to put the kids to bed."

"If you make your pieces shorter, you might get some airplay," said another.

"My God, I discovered you for myself—I don't want to hear you on the radio," said the fourth.

These friendly suggestions and self-conscious deliberations dampened my enthusiasm and inhibited my playing. With all of my "friends" now watching my progress with guarded concern, I feared that the second recording was being composed by everyone else but me.

Finally, after months of conscious deliberation and painstaking work, *Windsong* was done. With excitement and anticipation, the announcements went out and the orders came in. Soon, I thought, the accolades were sure to follow. But there was nothing. I had given my work to the world, but the world was not answering back. And when it did finally respond, it did so not with accolades but with returned tapes. First ten and then twenty *Windsong* tapes arrived back in the mail. More followed after that.

"Disappointing," one said.

"Not nearly as uplifting as the first," said another.

"It's so introspective that I find it depressing. How could you do this to us?" said a third.

I was about to conclude that my music career was over just as it had begun when someone called long-distance to thank me.

"This one is beautiful," he said, "so much more thoughtful and crafted than the last."

Another called to say the same.

"Disappointing."

"Beautiful."

"A letdown."

"Original."

I had planned a holiday to celebrate my success, but things had changed. I felt suddenly wistful now for that time not long past when nobody knew my name. I felt very tender inside, as if I were still forming myself. I was in the public eye now, and I realized how little I understood about fame. I postponed my holiday and went to a counselor for help instead.

"It's in the nature of your soul to create," he said to me. He was a composer and familiar with the territory I was exploring for the first time. "It's important to realize that your soul grows through your work in ways that have little relationship with sales or with failure or with outward success. And remember," he added, "whatever you are doing now is not your final task but simply a bridge to something else. Nothing is lost. As you are working on your art, you are also working on your life, and a life gains from everything; nothing goes to waste."

We talked of many things that day. He spoke of the hidden dangers of early success, of how, through our creations, we sometimes show the world the most vulnerable parts of ourselves before we are ready to receive and hold its sometimes thoughtless and critical response. "Some artists stop," he said. "We never hear from them again. Those who go on, however, somehow understand that their work represents something more than career building. It is their souls that they are forming. While they may work in the service of others, they are accountable to no one but the gods and themselves."

As I stood to leave, he added, "I know you may be feeling some pain now with the response to this work, but remember that after the eighth or tenth recording, you will have forgotten the reactions you received to the first few."

Ten! I said to myself as I stepped into the street. This was to be my last. There was room for two—well, perhaps three—but ten?

The choice of the title for *Windsong* had been appropriate in ways that I did not foresee at the time. The wind is dangerous; it blows how and where it will. It speaks of freedom; its gusts shake loose our old and tired structures that may impede our way. The wind is also a trickster, pulling apart our efforts to predict our lives. And, most important, it fans the flames that can sear and open our hearts. My music spoke of water and of flow. The response to *Windsong*, however, had also surfaced a bold determination, one that carried with it the elements of wind and fire. I believed that *Windsong* would be my last recording but, in time, so many others followed that it would not even be remembered as one of my first. "Do the thing," Emerson once said, "and you shall have the power." There was something more to be done here, not only about piano playing but also about me, and it involved staying on the bench.

When the winds strip us bare, the present moment is often the safest place to be. This is not a place of idle fantasies. When we bring all of our attention to this one moment in time, we engage in an intimate encounter with the origins of our own creative capacities.

"Being carried along is not enough," Rilke says to us. Instead, he invites us to be ambitious, to stretch the limits of our abilities, to not allow ourselves, or our work, to become too small. And yet, paradoxically, it is in the details or the particulars of our work, in sorting out these tensions of the opposites, that the origins of our inspiration are to be found.

What is the interplay, for example, in finding the balance between being too tentative or too bold; in defining the structure within a piece of music and, at the same time, letting it spontaneously unfold; in being careless one moment and in the next very controlled; in playing too fast and then too slow? The energy is not to be found in either direction, but in the middle. It is in learning to hold all of these contradictions, in trying to resolve them not by leaning one way or the next but by expanding into the possibilities that they might embrace, that we become attuned to ourselves and the world. Though I may often fail in the struggle to find and hold this middle ground, it is what I am searching for when I play.

This road, Rilke tells us, grows out in ever-widening circles. Each successive composition becomes a little broader, deeper, wider, and more expansive than the rest. It is found not through grand gestures but often in the smallest, most imperceptible and gentle steps. To look forward, it may seem that we're not moving at all. But when we look back, we are moving faster than the wind. The universe is not slow, and we are expanding outward at the speed of light. We will continue to do so as long as we are willing to live on the edge of the mystery, the wonder, the terror, the beauty, the sadness, and the joy. As Rilke says:

> Take your well-disciplined strengths
> and stretch them between two
>
> opposing poles. Because inside human beings
> is where God learns.
> (Trans. by Robert Bly)

Between the light and dark, and the heart and the head, between the in breath and out breath, between the science of the
music and its soul, lies the "'great song." Once heard, it cannot be
forgotten. Each recording since *Windsong* has been an exploration in
bringing these contrary forces into awareness—in my music and in
myself. When we engage directly in the dance between these divergent poles, our art becomes a living instrument through which
even the gods can benefit from the fruits of our work. In bringing
these opposites into a union within ourselves, we are also doing
the work of the world.

One Voice to Sing

From time to time, people approach me at the piano and ask me how I play. There is so much that might be said, and all of it seems so difficult to describe, that often I feel like a centipede who has just been asked to explain how it walks.

One evening after dinner, my friend David asked this same question. With strangers, I can usually feign silence, mumbling something about being an artist. But David was a friend and consulting client. So, with an effort, I tried to say something useful.

But I had no sooner begun than I realized that even with David I couldn't think of anything useful to say. "Is there anything specific you'd like to know?" I asked, hoping that if I stalled for time I might have an opportunity to focus my thoughts.

Then David started to talk. His question had really been a statement, and now that he began speaking, he had a lot to say.

"I have been trying to play the piano for a long time," he said.

"But I feel awkward with the keys. I've been trained to make sure that I've named each chord before moving on to the next. It's slow going, and I get frustrated and confused each time. It's really hard work. I don't think I'm improving and, probably most important, I'm not having much fun. For a time, I just believed that that was the way it was. But then I watch you, and you're just sitting there with your eyes closed and really enjoying yourself. How do you do it?"

I remembered my own struggles, trying to transform a few unexpected seconds of what felt to be genius into minutes and then hours of free play. What I enjoyed the most was shifting back and forth from composed music to freely created, spontaneous improvisations that flowed through my hands moment by moment. One form of music seemed to come from my head, the other from my heart. When I could learn to go back and forth freely between my heart and my head, especially on those days when I could be in both places at the same time, I felt I was opening a channel through which the music could flow. Of course, there were many dry days, when I felt that I played with no genius at all. Often, the inspiration came when I wasn't looking for it, when my back was turned or my focus was somewhere else. Once present, it had a life of its own; nothing could be added or taken away. For that moment, I couldn't imagine playing in any other way.

David had spent a lot time trying to master one form. Perhaps I could guide him into a direct experience of the other. "The territory we are exploring doesn't lend itself easily to explanation," I said to him. "As soon as the brain thinks it's got it, it shifts somewhere else. The primordial flame that sometimes ignites my playing is more in my hands than in my head. When I put too much effort into thinking about it or trying to locate and understand it, what I get back mostly is smoke. It is as Goethe once said: 'a mysterious power which everyone senses and no philosopher can explain.' So, why don't we go to the piano and play with it instead."

"If you think I'm going to play in front of you, you're crazy," David said, sinking more deeply into his seat and laughing nervously.

I smiled. I remembered how paralyzed I often felt when faced with the prospect of playing for another pianist.

"Listen!" I said. "This is not a performance. There are no wrong notes. It's an experiment. Think of it as a work in progress. Let's just take a few minutes now and explore this work together. There is nothing to do here; we'll just see what comes up."

Then I asked him to play, emphasizing that he not try to do anything special. His shoulders dropped a little. But I could tell by the way in which his fingers stiffly contacted the keys that this was not an easy thing for him to do.

He played from memory, his eyes focused in front of him as if there were music on the stand. The complex structures he worked within restricted his movements. Ideally, the forms and structures we create should support rather than impede our natural flow. But David somehow had this wired the other way around. It was obvious that he knew a lot about music; but listening to his struggles, I was reminded of D. H. Lawrence, who said, "We live in an excessively conscious age, we know so much, we feel so little."

Perhaps if I could leave him with one small gift this evening, it would be to help him feel the music. And as I considered how to pass this along to him, I wondered how it had worked for me. Often it came by noticing what attracted my curiosity. What was the *impulse* that most claimed my interest in that moment? Invariably, that interest led me into playing from what I didn't know—uncovering the invisible that lay beneath the visible, discovering something as simple and also as exciting as finding a new way of playing a familiar note. These discoveries came not only from searching for something new, but also from unlearning or forgetting what had gone before. In that moment of emptiness, the mind is open to a new possibility, like a renewal of innocence, a remembering of what attracted our interest to the instrument in the first place, the something that preceded our mastery of technique and chords. For each of us, it may be different; for me, it was in creating pictures with the music and simply loving the feel of the keys.

To guide David in the direction of hearing this sound field, I suggested that he keep his eyes closed for a while, listen to his breath, and then extend his attention to include the room. When I truly listen to my surroundings, I become more intimate with them. It opens my auditory imagination, creating a space through which something new can emerge. Whereas my vision involves going out to things, examining each in a separate, discrete, and sometimes fragmented way, my ears take in the world. It eases the critical nature of my mind and I become more engaged in the sounds of the world as something with which I want to play. When my playing feels forced and stiff, I close my eyes and follow my breathing. This brings me back to myself. I hoped that David, by listening to his music and being touched by his own work, might be penetrated by it as well.

Then David started to play. His transformation was startling to watch. I noticed it in his face first. The lines around his forehead relaxed, and his jaw dropped. Then I noticed how lightly his fingers danced across the keys. His eyes literally sparkled and his music, which was so measured before, was now filled with uninhibited joy. It was clear to me, and I hoped for him, that there was a musical voice inside him that clearly wanted to speak.

It was some time before David brought his music to an end. And unlike the abrupt stops that characterized his transitions before, his ending now was so deeply felt that even as his hands left the keys, a few notes hovered in the room. I can tell when the music is being formed in the head, because the room feels agitated; when it's flowing from the body as well, however, the room feels very still.

It was a long time before David was finally able to speak. Then he said very quietly, "Did I do *that?*"

"Yes," I replied.

"How?"

"I don't know."

"I felt like I was in a dream," he said. "Could I do that again?"

"Probably not quite," I answered, thinking about composer Gustav Mahler, who once said, "We cannot repeat a state of mind."

Sometimes we find ourselves in the presence of someone who has become larger than their carefully guarded worldly identities. These suddenly drop away, and they appear for a moment to be filled with a warmhearted, welcoming glow of life. That's how I experienced David that night.

But after our brief conversation, something changed. It seems hard to maintain this state when it comes to expressing it in words. Our language fails us: The more we try to find mental concepts to account for it, the more our conversation begins to speed up. How can we stay close to this vulnerable place, I wondered, and let it be shared not only in music but also in words? No sooner had I asked the question of myself than David unwittingly offered a response. He sat back, his shoulders tensed a little, and the familiar frown formed on his brow.

"I'll never do *that* again," he said finally.

"Why?" I asked, surprised at his sudden reversal.

"Because I have never felt that much out of control."

We sat together for a while longer before he had to go.

It is true that just beyond our threshold of consciousness, there exists a world more wondrous, terrifying, and magnificent than we can imagine. It is in fact another part of ourselves. But when we meet this part, even for an instant, as David had that night, another part of us contracts in fear; it doesn't want to lose precedence. To give ourselves over to this new self involves a faithfulness to something that lives outside the pursuit of our carefully constructed plans and goals. Instead, it involves acknowledging the presence of an underlying design, one that carries us forward with such inevitability that it confuses even our most careful calculations. It is like an insistent current that draws us ever closer to those tasks that only we can perform. On the days when I am fulfilling this task at the piano, and in my life, I am never quite in control.

For a moment, David had stepped over that threshold and connected with this passion. Although it may have taken him by surprise, like some strange and alien being, it was, in fact, simply that other part of himself. It remains quite near to us, but it is so beautiful and terrifying at the same time that often we will do everything in our power to deny that it is there. For once it explodes into our awareness, we realize how much we have sacrificed to avoid feeling it. This awareness can play havoc with our professional lives and cause us great pain.

David was paid to push. His company, through its policies and procedures, seemed to almost unwittingly inhibit this natural life-force rather than encourage its flow. Like most institutions, it had no appreciation that any other dimension of life existed beyond itself. But for a brief moment, David glimpsed this other world. And unlike the one he was familiar with, where force and effort had the greatest impact, in this other world it is the subtlest of actions that often have the greatest effect. David had received a call, an invitation to let some aspect of his life be guided, to allow himself to be told what to do, to trust an urging deeper and more profound than anything he had ever known and, in so doing, to become who he most passionately was. It is an invitation that, if accepted, involves sacrificing some aspect of who we have always believed we are.

David often spoke proudly of how in his organization he had power and control; but power seeks its security from *outside*; it finds comfort in the belief that it functions in a fixed and immutable universe. In his time with me at the piano, he had experienced the pleasure that beauty brings, beauty that finds its source from *within* itself, that moves in an ever-changing, ephemeral, chaotic, and turbulent field.

Power and beauty are antithetical. Power strives to build stable structures that can exist for all of time, while beauty shifts the earth from beneath our feet; as soon as we glimpse it, it is already gone. Between the two, I choose beauty, for when has power, unless it is used in the service of beauty, ever been able to create anything of permanence in the world? "It is beauty," Emerson once said, "not power, that is our true guide, leading us in the directions we must go in order to discover whatever it is we are uniquely intended to know." For a moment, David had connected with this beauty; it had breathed its life into his, and even though he might step back, his world would never be quite the same again.

But perhaps David had been wise to be cautious. "We go to heaven for form," William Blake once said, "but we go to hell for energy." Often, our first contact with the vastness of this beauty is through our fear. As Rilke once said, "The breadth of this energy seems so alien and so opposed to us that our brain disintegrates at the point where we force ourselves to think about it." We create structures and routines so that we won't feel it, yet it continues to live in the shadows, intruding itself upon us with the sudden halting of the breath, the hollow feeling deep in the chest, or the unexpected racing of our pulse during some quiet moment of the day, or, even more often, late at night, when we are less defended.

"We have become accustomed to smaller things," Rilke says to us. "This is our energy, all *our* energy, which is still too strong for us. It is true that we don't know it," he continues, "but aren't we most ignorant about what is most our own?"

How, we wonder, are we able to make this energy our own? Is it possible, as Rilke says, that that which most belongs to us is also that which we least understand? Being at the piano has offered me a way in. For example, when it is inspiration I want, I play the high notes, but if it is more energy that I am seeking, I go instead to the low bass tones. To find the resonance and depth in these tones, I drop into them, merging with the keys, letting the physical impulse from my body be my guide. What was it about the piano that allowed me to be with it in this way? I had a relationship with it: I didn't feel victimized when I hit a wrong note or when things didn't work out in a particular way. I trusted that, regardless of the outcome, this was where I belonged. This trust is found in the intimacy I feel with the instrument each time I touch the keys. It asks me to be curious and attentive with it, to appreciate that the music, like the energy behind it, is a constantly fluid and changing thing. The piano invites me to engage with it. If I stand back or become too detached, I find that I am being left behind.

Can we work with fear the same way? Is it possible to have a relationship with it? Can we get closer to it, probe into it, feel its color, its edges, and its weight? Is it possible to merge with and observe its movement and trust that if we accept it into our lives, it will also dissolve into something else? Can we let our entire lives be improvisations so that we can come into a direct encounter with whatever is moving in us without filtering through the programs we have acquired based on what we've been told to believe? I think Emerson said that much of what goes on in our mind is none of our business. Yet I could sense that David had suddenly been possessed by thoughts, ones that said to him: You cannot play like this; the experience you have just had does not exist. These thoughts, often unformed and unexamined, rule our lives. They were powerful enough to bring David to a stop.

So often we use these thoughts of judgment and control as a first line of defense when we notice deeper feelings pushing at the door. Yet inside these feelings lies the source of our true spirit, a willing and creative impulse that wants to be allowed to flow through us. If we open to it, gradually we will find renewed strength in some of the softer dimensions of experience, allowing feelings like reverence, vulnerability, openness, and appreciation to enter our lives.

David wavered for a time. Occasionally, we talked about how he might integrate his love for music into his life. Ultimately, he accepted a job promotion instead. He called me several weeks later to

tell me why. More money was the reason, he explained, and the possibility that if he played his cards right, he might get a vice-president position in five years and an even greater and more influential international role in the company in perhaps ten. I was saddened by our conversation. I was familiar with both worlds and I knew by the sound of his voice that he had given in to the part of his mind that was so fearful for his future security. He allowed this concern to distract him from exploring the greater love that was contained within. What had I to offer him instead but a chance to become a musical poet, sitting comfortably cloaked and alone under some fragrant blossoming tree with nothing but his lyre and infinite space with which to explore some invisible realm and, perhaps in some far future, to bring back what he had found there for all of us to hear? Poet

Michael Blumenthal writes in his poem "A Man Lost by a River":

There is a voice inside the body,

There is a voice And a music,
a throbbing, four chambered pear
that wants to be heard, that sits
alone by the river with its mandolin
and its torn coat, and sings
for whomever will listen
a song that no one wants to hear.

But sometimes, lost,
on his way to somewhere significant,
a man in a long coat, carrying
a briefcase, wanders into the forest.

He hears the voice and mandolin,
he sees the thrush and the dandelion,
and the mist rising from the river.

And his life is never the same,
for having been lost—
for having strayed from the path of his routine,
for no good reason.

What is that voice by the river? How do we step from the path of our routine in order to hear it? What would it mean to follow its song, even if it is something that no one else wants to hear?

Following this voice doesn't mean we have to give up or change our day jobs. Our art does not need to be our career. But sometimes we cannot be reasonable about it either. Our lives deserve something more. If we are to find the vastness of this beauty and love for ourselves, each of us needs time to wander aimlessly and perhaps fearfully into the forest. What if I become lost and cannot find my way back? we might ask. When I begin to feel that fear, I remind myself that perhaps the only time we are truly lost is when we ignore these deeper impulses and insist that achieving a narrow set of goals related only to meeting the bottom line and accomplishing the end result can offer a satisfying life.

Yielding to this call to our imaginative life may take many forms. For some people it may involve simply doing their work in a more mindful way or creating a time and space in their day to do something that truly brings them pleasure or allows them to express their love in a new way. One person I knew left her job to fulfill a lifelong dream to return to school, get her certificate and teach math. For another, it involved bringing home a sick dog and nursing it back to health.

No matter how distant the call may sound, that person by the river is no stranger to us. We have met this voice before and we will feel its absence in our lives until the time comes when we are willing to meet with it again. Often, it is difficult to hear this voice amidst the busyness and fragmentation of our everyday world. And though responding to its call may change our lives in ways we cannot foresee, we can trust that it won't narrow or diminish our lives in the ways we might expect. It fact, it is this voice that offers the possibility of a future of ongoing generativity rather than despair. It reminds us that the world is there to welcome us when we are willing to take the first step. David had taken that one step and perhaps, in time, he would take all the rest. It is a step of faithfulness, of saying to no one in particular that we trust, as Gaston Bachalard did, that, "the Universe . . . beyond all its miseries, has a destiny of happiness." It is our birthright to reencounter paradise in whatever form it takes for us.

Everywhere We Are Is Called Home

A friend was teaching a group of native women in a remote northern Ontario community. Each time she asked a question there was a long silence. After a time, this began to confuse and annoy her. She was accustomed to fast-paced conversations, in which ideas bounced quickly around the room like tennis balls. Finally her frustration reached a peak.

"Why does it take you so long to answer my questions?" she asked.

Once again, there was a long silence. She was about to repeat the question when one of the women said, "We don't speak alone; we are waiting for the spirit to speak through us."

Often, when I sit at the piano I am also waiting for the spirit to speak. It comes in those moments of pure play, when I am free of agendas or goals or motives and can simply enter into the pure joy of creation itself. The past and future drop away. I feel myself immersed in a field of sensation—listening, breathing, touching, smelling, waiting, feeling. This is a space of free and open attention, of infinite possibility, where anything can happen.

One day, I took this cue and wondered if I could apply it to the rest of my life as well. Was it possible to engage in what Rilke speaks of as the real task, which is to "listen to the news that is always arriving out of silence"? There was very little silence in my event-driven life. Each time I glanced at my schedule book, all I saw was ink.

It came to awareness first one hot August afternoon as Judy and I sat by the lake at our summer cottage and talked about our life. The water was still, as was the air. It seems easier to talk about creating chaos in your life when there is so little of it in you. This was one of those moments—quiet, pristine, peaceful—the generosity of the universe was behind us, and everything seemed possible.

It began with the idea of selling the house. We would also let go of our consulting practice and travel for a while. In saying these words, I felt a slight tremor deep inside, like the smallest hint of great plates shifting beneath the surface. I felt a little light-headed; I thought it might be the intense sun that day, but it was something else. We were talking about dropping through the floorboards, rearranging some of the fundamental props that had given a foundation and structure to our life. Perhaps truly worthwhile decisions, the ones that can't be explained on reasonable grounds, begin this way. They aren't easily reduced to words. They flow instead from some deeper truth that lies beyond the intellect's ability to explain or understand. Yet, once acted upon, there is often an effortlessness to the way things unfold. This was such a decision.

Within two weeks, our house was listed on the real-estate market. Four days later, it was sold. Six weeks later, we returned to the cottage. The furniture and boxes that could not fit inside now stood like ghostly sentinels scattered beneath the trees under a light dusting of snow.

The next day a storm blew up. Strong gusts buffeted the cottage and whipped up the lake. Gray, angry, foaming waters lashed the beach where we had sat so peacefully two months before. I love weather. The elements that had been a backdrop to my busy schedule just a few weeks before were now in the foreground of my life. But the fierceness of this wind unsettled me.

This did not feel like just another autumn storm. Rather, it was a test of my faith. The dark clouds sat heavy in the sky. They were like a mirror, reflecting back to me my own emerging doubts and fears. Why were we doing this? What compelled us to leave so much that was familiar?

"What are you going to do?" our friends asked.

"Nothing," was our only reply.

How was it possible that a step that had seemed so clear and certain one calm sunny day could be so mired in uncertainty the next? The gusts whipped around me, ripping away the few remaining leaves from the trees. As I watched them scurry and disappear in the driving wind, my own familiar moorings felt torn from me as well. "Our nature lies in movement," says Blaise Pascal. "Complete calm is death." Perhaps it was this truth that explained our inner restlessness—the urge, despite our misgivings, to suddenly dismantle the life that we had so carefully planned.

At the piano, I have always taken pleasure in following this inner movement. To find it I often dropped what I was doing and veered to the left. It involved getting lost for a while, exploring new and unfamiliar ground, feeling around the edges of things and stepping outside the familiar world of form. A forester once told me that in the forest, the nutrients are to be found at the edges of places, such as where hardwoods change to softwoods or the thick forest changes to meadow. I felt that I was nourished in the same way, not by being either inside or outside the composition, but somewhere between form and formless, in that place Novalis describes at the seat of the soul.

I remembered, as a child, how the stories I heard and read also had this quality. They were told at night, close to the fire and near the boundaries of the dark forest. Each word then was rich with meaning and anticipation. The stakes were high in these stories: The hero could have lost it all; the future could not be clearly seen or foretold. It was this very absence of clarity, this sense of mistiness or darkness, that gave wings to the words and assured me that the story would never grow old.

By allowing myself to live at the edge of this uncertainty, I also created an opening for something new to come. I wanted the questions, not the answers, the mystery, not the solutions; I wanted conversation with my life, not merely a monologue. Unless all of these elements came together, there was no one who could participate in my life but me.

In the evenings, Judy and I walked the road close to the shore of the lake. I felt the crunch of the gravel underfoot and the comfort and warmth of her hand in mine. "Travel with a candle, not a flashlight," a city friend had advised us before we left. I thought of this candle now as we felt our way along the road. I had forgotten how dark it was in the country at night. In the absence of any firm plans or goals to focus on, our lives had become very much like the candle. Its melting wax felt like it was burning off any preconceived ideas about who we were or what we should be. We, too, now danced on the edge of extinction, feeling each moment expand and then give way to the next, as we learn to walk in an unlit world.

In the city, bold lights filled the nights, their glow penetrating the sky and obscuring the stars. There, I was conditioned to associate anything related to darkness as being unsafe. Living in a constant state of artificial illumination, I became uneasy when anything in my life began to fade. I felt a sadness for the life I was leaving behind. Now that I had put aside the important projects and the colleagues that had defined me, was there really anything of me left? How soon would I be forgotten? In that moment, I realized how ephemeral *all* of those things were. Ideas like competence, success, and competition seemed remote now. It was hard to believe how quickly concepts that had represented the bedrock of my life faded from view.

A chill ran through me. The moon and the darkness felt both dangerous and strangely comforting. Together, they were beginning to dissolve some of the edges of my fast-paced and spirited life. I was grateful now for these precious moments when I could not see or be seen. I had to soften my vision in order to feel my way along the darkened road. Even this simple act was helping me to come more into alignment with the natural cycles of things, cycles that might now have a greater bearing on how I lived my life. These cycles were not easy to find in the city. The natural ebb and flow of light and dark, of the in breath and the out breath, never came. It knew little of rest, of receiving, of allowing the

natural current of things to have a place. Corporate life kept finding new ways of penetrating every dimension of my life. Now,
listening to the crunch of gravel underfoot, finding myself free of
all agendas and plans, I realized how subtly I had given myself
away. I had lost all sense of personal time, its boundaries forever
eroded with the construction of each new office tower, with the
erection of every brightly flashing multicolored neon sign. Donut
shops, banking machines, and convenience stores had stolen away
the night.

The possibility of forming a very different kind of life felt overwhelming. I understood now why we might so willingly imprison
ourselves in restrictive relationships or jobs. For with my emerging freedom also came an immense responsibility. Whatever
choices I made now, I had only myself to blame.

As we turned to walk back to the cottage and warm ourselves
by the fire in the stove, my body shuddered again with the excitement and the cold. I remembered several words from a poem by
Rilke and imagined that for a moment I felt a little as he did when
he said, "It is possible a great energy is moving near me. I have
faith in nights."

We bought a van. As the days grew shorter, we carefully chose
those items that we most wanted. Then, after hours of trial and
error, we reluctantly divided this list in two, and then divided it
into two again. The Catholic mystic teacher Meister Eckhart once
said, "The soul grows through subtraction, not addition." As we
saw our large, spacious home reduced to a seasonal cottage, and
now to a small travel van, I was sure that our souls would grow
well this winter.

One warm, sunny day in late November, I was stacking wood.

I looked at the clear blue sky and then over to the lake, which was absolutely still. This is beautiful, I thought. Perhaps we'll stay here, warm ourselves by the fire, and read travel books all winter!

But then, as the sudden damp chill of a southeast wind rustled the few remaining dry leaves on the nearby trees, I remembered how my great-uncle, an experienced weather forecaster, always said that the lake was this still just before a big storm. That night, the wind howled and the temperature dropped. By morning, twelve inches of snow had fallen. We felt like caterpillars entering the chrysalis. The journey that lay ahead might change us so significantly that we wouldn't know ourselves on our return. Hopefully, we would be transformed into butterflies. But regardless of the outcome, the cold and snow were signaling that it was time to leave. Within a few days, the cottage was locked and the van was packed. We were on our way.

Six days later, we arrived in Florida. There, we continued south to Key Largo. As soon as we entered the campground, we took a moment to meet our neighbors and discover what exotic part of the country they had come from.

"Big Cedar," they said proudly.

"Near Orillia?" I asked with dismay.

"Yep."

Our first contacts lived three miles from home.

Soon we traveled back up the coast. We had a wonderful time meeting new friends who, in turn, introduced us to others along the way. But finally, a concert date pointed us toward Houston and other points west.

As we entered west Texas, the verdant terrain of the Southeast now turned flat, brown, and gray. The absence of any variation in the external landscape amplified an inner sense of growing despair. That evening, we pulled into a KOA campground. It was winter in the desert—the cold wind chilled our bodies, the grit and sand stung our eyes. The following morning, we woke up cold and stiff and sore. As I looked across the empty miles of rock, sand, and rangeland, I grieved the absence of old friends, a time clock, and the opportunity to wear a suit and go to a real job. I was lost. The first question I asked as I stepped from the van was, "Where are we, what are we doing, and why are we *here?*"

I had taken pride in my many identities, activities, and accomplishments. They were the moorings that anchored me to solid ground. But here on these open and endless rangelands, I had nothing to do, nowhere to go, and nobody to be. I no longer knew who I was. I had nothing to cling to, not even a tree.

The van had always felt like a womb, offering the possibility of new life. But as we turned to go deeper into the desert, it felt more like a tomb. It was taking me farther from any life I had ever known. We felt trapped with ourselves and with each other. Our adventure, which had been conceived in heaven, now felt like a journey from hell.

The tension is often greatest just before letting go. Doubt and confusion serve as the guardians, protecting the entrance to the inner realms, discouraging us from blindly following the more mysterious and unpredictable urgings of our hearts. Yet my heart could be trusted. It seemed to know where it was going, even if my mind did not comprehend. Slowly, we headed farther west until eventually, we did reach the sea.

There, high on a misty narrow plateau with the coastal ridge of the Santa Lucia Mountains behind me and the surf of the Pacific

Ocean pounding at my feet, I stood at the edge of what Chilean poet Pablo Neruda speaks of as the "heartbeat of the universe." Among the roar of these great swells, I heard the ancient origins from which my music had come. As I stood on the cliff, soaked in the vastness of this beauty, I felt the cells of my body expanding wider and wider until I thought I might burst.

The universe reveals itself to us through sounds we are familiar with—the roar of the surf, the hollow wind blowing through a leafless forest, the thin layers of ice forming on a lake on a cold December morning, the way that words resonate in a poem—each of these is like a drumbeat calling us back to our true home. The more that we expand in response to these sounds, the more that is offered to us and the more we can pass along. Standing close to these waters helped me see that the next steps in my life would need to be taken with a full and open heart, one strong enough to educate my intellect to embrace these new unfolding dimensions that my mind found difficult to accept.

Now when I sat at the piano, I listened for how the music had changed. The tones came not only in the arrangement of notes and chords, but in waves, the sounds washing over me like the surging waters of the sea that lay close to my feet.

We returned to the cottage in the spring and remained through the winter that followed. Though we had planned to return to the coast, as the leaves turned from green to a fiery red and gold, I realized how much I missed winter. I enjoyed its snowy silence, the trees and lakes and fields, and dark, frost-filled nights. This journey had been more than just traveling America's open and winding roads. By setting aside, even for an instant, a certain future for an outrageous present, we had become gypsies on what

Walt Whitman speaks of as one of the "roads for traveling souls."

When I am on this road, I feel like I am living a gypsy life. It becomes difficult to hang onto any one thing for long; whatever I grasp for safety turns to stone. The past and the future enfold into a larger present. There is comfort here, even if the images of the future hover like mysterious and shadowy forms just beyond the candle's light. Beneath it all, I can trust that no matter in what form my actions flow, if they are warmed by the wishes of my heart, whatever I create along this road will hold. Then I can be assured that the world is a reflection of me, and that everywhere I am can be called home.

Finding a Musical
Intelligence

"I sense the name Fred around and about you," the tarot card reader said. "Who's Fred?"

The question caught me off guard.

"Sorry," I replied thoughtfully to the woman sitting across the table from me. "I don't know any Freds."

She had been recommended by a friend. Although I had found readings of this nature helpful in the past, I was a little tentative. However much I loved to enter into a dance with the invisible realms when I played the piano, I was always a little uneasy when someone else began tuning into them to foresee patterns and events in my life.

Then she sat still for the longest time, the tarot deck spread in front of her. Suddenly, she clapped her hands and opened her eyes wide.

I jumped.

"Chopin!" she said, her voice clear and precise. "Does the name Frédéric Chopin mean anything to you?"

"Ahh, yes," I sputtered. The sudden weakness in my voice didn't come close to matching the excitement in my chest.

Chopin. How could she have known that my decision to make music my career had been made the day after I had first heard the music of Chopin? I was quite sure that she didn't even know I was a pianist.

"Chopin," I repeated slowly under my breath, my voice a whisper now. "I love Chopin."

"Good," she said briskly and businesslike. "I'm glad we cleared that up."

But what had now been "cleared up" for her had released a flood of memories for me.

I recalled the winter afternoons at the college conservatory. Of how, when I opened the music book to Chopin, my teacher would step away from the piano and take a seat by the window. There, he listened quietly to the music in a state that he once described as reverie. Although his penciled corrections to my interpretations of Bach and Beethoven filled the page, when we turned to the music of Chopin he had nothing but praise. Then my memories drifted even farther back, to the Saturday afternoon I went to see the film called *The Eddie Duchin Story*. Tyrone Power acted the role of pianist Eddie Duchin while Carmen Cavallero played the piano. The film opened with Power/Cavallero playing the Chopin nocturne in E-flat minor.

I had sat mesmerized, my popcorn untouched, my eyes glistening with tears. I had never heard a piano played quite that way before. I now knew that this instrument could open and soothe my heart as well as train my ears.

The experience of Chopin penetrated deep into some protected layer of my being after that day. There it remained, forgotten like a fragile ember through the years of baseball, soccer, and long nights performing the music of Little Richard, Floyd Cramer, and Fats Domino, and then many more years of graduate school and career building, before it appeared again.

Perhaps the seeds that define our gifts and our destiny are planted this way. Our heart is seared for a moment in childhood, and then the inspiration is gone. We are protected from our impulse to go directly into its intense heat for fear that we would become initiated into adulthood too soon. Years pass. Slowly we spiral around this inspiration until such a time as we are ready to receive it. Only then do we find the key, the knowledge of how to fan this ember into flame.

The key, in this instance, was the recognition and confirmation from another who heard an echo of Chopin in my work.

Discovering how to join his voice with mine, however, could not be achieved through playing the notes on the page. It was the *spirit* of Chopin's work that I wanted, and that heartfelt and poetic feeling could come only from inside of me. To find it, I had to set aside the many ways that I could be clever at the piano and suspend my vision for the accomplishment of great works. Instead, I engaged in a search for that one note that had truth and meaning, the one note that I could claim held to the spirit of Chopin's music but which was truly my own. It was through listening closely for the feeling in the notes and exploring the conversation that emerged between the left hand and the right that I felt Chopin's spirit manifest in my playing. He was teaching me through my fingers; I felt his touch in my hands.

"He is your muse," my card reader said by way of clarifying my relationship with Chopin. "His soul is connected to yours. But it is nothing to be uncomfortable about. This has been going on for some time. You are deeply affected by his influence, even if you are not conscious of it. But nothing is about to change. What I am offering you is simply a clarification of something that has been going on all along."

Several days after the tarot reading, I was browsing through the music section of a downtown bookstore. There, I picked up a book about Chopin's teaching methods as described through the accounts of his students and friends. The letters fascinated me.

"Go for long walks, visit museums, or read a good book," Chopin said repeatedly. This, he was convinced, was more beneficial to the suppleness of the music than the "mental numbness" that was caused by the long hours of strenuous and mechanical practice. It would also give his students the naturalness and simplicity he wanted to hear in their playing. "The fingers should always fall lightly and freely on the notes," he insisted. "They should never be forced."

Chopin looked more for poise in his students' playing than for effort. Throughout his teaching, it was the delicacy of the notes that took precedence over technical virtuosity. What he wanted his students to master above all was the *art of touch*. "Caress the key, never bash it," he would say emphatically. And he always encouraged his students to mold the note with a velvet hand rather than strike it, to feel and sink into it, as if immersing themselves in the depths of the piano.

Students said that he would repeat without ceasing: "Easily, easily!" Suppleness was his great object. Stiffness exasperated him. To find this ease, he said to his students, "Express as you feel . . . I give you full authority to do whatever you want; follow freely the ideal you've set for yourself and which you must feel within you."

For Chopin, simplicity was the hardest thing, but for him it was also the only thing. The beautiful quality of sound he sought after could be found only through being relaxed at the keyboard. Music was poetry for Chopin. It was, therefore, through the discipline of finding just the right word or image, and well as through music, that he tried to develop a language in which the sound production or the art of touch always took precedence over the acquisition of virtuosity.

As I read these passages, my body remembered the feel of his music, even though my mind may have forgotten the notes. I also recalled a conversation I had had with a friend a few months before.

"What is your musical intelligence?" he asked.

"Intelligence?" I said. I didn't know I had one. Often, I believed that I played with no intelligence at all. I rarely knew which chord I was on, let alone which one I had come from, or where I was going next. I played more from feeling than forethought, and I was more drawn to the free flow of the music than to holding to any fixed ideas. My interest was in finding that fine edge at the piano where I could no longer tell whether I was moving the music or it was moving me. It was intuition and instinct that guided my hands as much as reflection or analysis. I was convinced that there were rich musical images hidden beneath the keys. I used my hands to carefully separate the wet, dark loam in order to uncover some hidden tributary. It was the process of discovering and following this, wherever it might lead, that filled me with the most joy.

There was a discipline here as well. It came in learning how to let the notes sing, in discovering how to master the way the finger touched the key, rather that striking it. It required concentration and careful listening to myself as I tried to shape and mold the tone of the note just right. It involved letting go—learning how to let the music take free flight within the context of an ever-changing form. And, most of all, it involved respecting my limits: knowing that my progress at the piano could not be pushed, staying within my own technical range, and appreciating that if I stayed close to the music that gave me the most pleasure and for which I felt the most passion, it would flow without strain.

But to find this quality of touch in the piano, I also had to find it within myself. It was not easy. Playing this way involves engaging in a dialogue with oneself, penetrating beneath the surface and consciously engaging with those parts of myself that find this work too hard and invent any number of reasons for why they do not want to go further. But I also learned that I could rely on other parts of myself that could override these concerns. Once I made this commitment to myself, other forces set to work, ones that transcended and augmented my own. So often when I returned to the piano, I was grateful to find that somehow further elaboration had taken place, with even more efficiency, when I wasn't around. Once I set things in motion, much of it got worked out while I was doing something else. So I balanced my piano practice with time spent going for long walks, visiting art museums, and reading good books.

For many years, my business consulting practice offered a cover through which I could engage directly with the world and still preserve a protected space for this deeper work. It is easy to feel profoundly vulnerable and self-conscious, even embarrassed, when we begin penetrating the deeper layers of who we are, even when we know that the qualities being released from within us may prove to be our greatest strengths. The nature of this inner movement can be both confusing and frightening. I can feel myself engaged in a process of unfolding that is not entirely of my own making. Each time I attempt to take charge of it, it is gone. Yet when I am being sincere in this work, I can trust that even though I may feel more fragile and vulnerable than I have ever felt before, I am, in fact, also stronger, because this work, even when I feel it is tearing me apart, is also allowing me to become more deeply rooted in a sense of who I am.

In the words of David Whyte's poem "Out on the Ocean":

> . . . and the spark behind fear
> recognized as life
> leaps into flame
>
>
>
> always this energy smoulders inside
> when it remains unlit
> the body fills with dense smoke.

What is contained in that fragile ember that burns quietly in my own soul? What needs to be forgotten for this ember to be fanned into flame? Where are the edges where I feel most vulnerable? Is it possible that these areas might also be the source of my greatest strengths?

These questions offered a way in, a reminder that I am not searching for simply one frame of mind. Instead, I wanted to deepen my connection with that underground river that will always bring forth new and different ideas each time. But this is delicate work. I remember a friend who, upon hearing this in her own playing, immediately set about to record it. She hired an agent, developed a marketing plan, worked out an album cover design, retained a sound engineer, and moved her grand piano into a studio. But when she finally sat down to play, the subtle magic that had been in the music was gone. There is a shyness to this energy that guides our work. When we shine the light of celebrity upon it, it is suddenly nowhere to be found. And what replaces it is often a poor substitute. Perhaps this is why so many great teachers and artists have refused to create any long-standing permanent record of their work. It is a tribute to each particular moment only, a gift for those who are there, a blessing for the gods.

To find this purity of expression, one free of self-serving intentions or goals, we may also find ourselves engaged in other work, sometimes for many years, before we become involved in an art form. For example, my partner Judy is able to apply long, beautiful, and natural brush strokes to the canvas. Others wonder how she is able to do this. It is because for many years she did body massage, work that helped her learn how to lead from her body. But for those many years as a masseuse she did not know where it might lead.

This "not knowing" may serve us well, because as soon as we

try to capture and preserve this spirit, we inevitably enter in a struggle with that other part of ourselves that tries to complicate it and force this spirit to serve its own ends. This complicating part of ourselves is quick to step into the river, but soon finds itself out of its depth and begins swimming the wrong way. Stubbornly, we try to go against the current, based upon the conviction that we must conquer and control these forces because it is our destiny to have our own way.

Yet evolution has taught us something different. It has not only been those strong, stubborn species that survived, but also their frail cousins with their thin bones who, through their sensitive and responsive connection to their world, found a delicate balance with the earth. Finding the spirit of Chopin inside my music involved cultivating this same delicate balance within myself. In this balance I am invited to probe things with the wonder and caring of a child or a lover. It's to hold my work lightly in order to respect and be responsive to the music's ever-changing form.

What in your life might you be attached to that you need to hold more lightly? What is it you are called to follow, even when it feels like you are following the free and erratic flight of a wild bird?

Sometimes, when I am lost and there is nowhere to turn, I step away from the bench. I go for a long walk or I listen to a Chopin nocturne. His music fills the room, a reminder that I am simply "God's flute." I serve the great musician; it is His music playing through me. Rumi says:

Love plays and plays and is the music played . . .
Let that musician finish the poem . . .
I am a waterbird flying into the sun.

When the search for our own truth is our work, we become the waterbird flying into the sun. I return to the piano; my fingers rest in the keys. There are not just two hands on the piano now, there are four. Chopin has joined me on the bench again.

Living What We Love

Several years ago, I joined a group of colleagues on a rope course. The program was designed to help us face our fears and surpass our limitations. For some, it was easy to climb forty feet in the air on a rope and with a great whoop swing quickly and gracefully to the ground. But for others, including me, the fear of being paralyzed on a rope ladder high in the air was immobilizing. I was haunted by images of sitting frozen, clutching a branch high up in one of the tall trees, perhaps for days.

Later, walking back to camp, a friend asked: "Michael, what experience in your life would be equivalent to climbing the high ropes?" Without a moment of hesitation, I replied, "Doing a solo piano concert."

Sometime after this conversation, I received a call.

"Would you be interested in performing a concert for us this spring?" a voice said over the phone. The request involved performing for a large audience as part of an International Piano Festival in Montreal.

For a moment, I imagined that this was my friend from the rope course. Sure, I thought. Now from high atop a platform forty feet up in the sky . . . we present Michael Jones playing his Concert Bosendorfer. . . . But this was no time for humor; I was being presented with a serious request. Most of the other performances would be based on a classical repertoire, he explained, but they wanted something a little different for their last night. That's when they wanted me to perform.

I had never performed in front of a large group of strangers before. The spontaneous improvisations I had become known for were almost always done in small recitals or with close friends in the privacy of my own home. How could I know in advance how my feelings might affect the music? I wondered. What if I had a cold or the flu and was not in the mood to play at all? What if the muse that so often inspired my work in ways that I did not understand were somewhere else that night? How many variations could I perform on just one song if nothing else came to mind and I still had several long hours to fill?

These fears began causing me sleepless nights. I decided that for this concert, I could not play as I usually did; the stakes were too high. Instead, I had better take this one seriously. I would have to have a *plan*. To prepare, I spent the next weeks and months imagining myself playing in front of a group of people. The first day, I had five in the room. Then I added five more. Several weeks later, I added a few more. By the week of the concert, I was up to one thousand. They sat on the floor, others leaned against the wall, some were on the deck outside, and still others were on the street and looking in through the windows. By the night of the performance, I was ready to play!

That evening as I stood backstage, a member of the coordinating committee said that the hall was filling quickly. "There are many music teachers who signed up for the series this year," he said enthusiastically. "They will be among your audience tonight as well." As soon as I heard the words "music teachers," something shifted inside. I realized that I was not ready to play this concert after all.

A few minutes later as I stepped out onto the large, empty stage, I was engaged in an act of courage that was greater than I knew. As I glanced across the packed and darkened theater, a terror rose up to meet me that lifted me right off my feet. I remembered the piano recitals I had given as a child, the panels of judges with their stern and unforgiving glances, their pens scribbling furiously on their scorecards as I played. And I remembered their dispassionate looks as I walked away from the piano, sometimes after the piece was finished, sometimes before, but each time feeling that I had died on the stage. I imagined that they were there still, sitting in the front row, their faces cold and expectant as they watched me sit, reluctant and trembling now, on the piano stool.

What had I to give in this formal atmosphere that had any true value? I wondered. As these thoughts took hold, my hands began to tremble even more. At least my feet are still, I said to myself with some relief. But no sooner had I said this than they began to shake as well. I had been invited here to relax this audience, I thought, but who is going to relax me?! I felt an immediate impulse to retreat backstage, but I wasn't confident now that I could walk the twenty feet that separated me from possible salvation. Instead, I checked my watch. Two minutes had passed; only eighty-eight minutes remained in the performance.

In that moment when I believed that all was lost, another memory came to mind—the afternoon I sat nervously filling out forms in the security room of a state penitentiary.

"It's just a minimum-security facility," a member of the organizing committee had said over the phone several weeks before. "There is no reason to be concerned."

But as we walked to the gate and looked at the high walls with barbed wire and guard towers, I realized that I had good reason to be concerned after all. I signed a waiver acknowledging that I was entering dangerous territory and in so doing released the state of Ohio of any responsibility for my safety. Then I was processed through three security checkpoints and walked with the guards up a wide hallway. A large group of prisoners, perhaps a hundred or so, came out of the cafeteria and walked toward us, moving slowly to the sides as we walked by. Soon we reached the chapel and stepped inside.

Fifty or sixty men packed into the hot, stuffy chapel that afternoon. The room was noisy and full, the piano dull and old. Most of its notes were badly out of tune.

I had played for just five minutes or so when a muscular, heavy-set man in the front row stood up and squeezed past two others. Then he turned and walked slowly down the middle aisle and out the door. It banged shut; then everything was still.

I felt shaken by his abrupt departure. With one eye on the piano now and the other on the door, I wondered how long it would take for the rest to follow. I felt awkward and out of place.

How soon would it take for me to finish this concert and get out of this place?

Sometime later the door opened again. The same man stepped through and walked slowly up to the piano. He stood beside me for a time, then, carefully, he set a glass of water on the ledge beside the keys. Then he returned to his seat. I was suddenly overcome with a warm rush of gratitude, and a little bit of guilt. In bringing me this glass of water, this man had given me something else. I realized that I was not in this thing alone. I was an instrument for some broader purpose, not to simply fulfill my own ends. In that moment, I came to feel that wherever I was, it was where I belonged. Why I was in this place and not somewhere else was not something I needed to try to figure out. There was nothing to fear. The piano, which had felt listless before, suddenly felt crisp and full. The notes now seemed strangely in tune; the sounds filled the hall.

I remembered the night before I played in the prison; I had performed a concert at a reception and meeting for a group of art patrons at the local university. All the men were dressed in tuxedos. It was a formal affair in which everything had to be done just right. The piano was set beside four large floor-to-ceiling windows, which looked out upon a magnificent pink magnolia tree in full bloom. After playing for five minutes or so, I glanced out of the window. There, under the rich canopy of blossoms for all to see, were two rabbits mating in the grass, their activities clearly evident to the entire audience in the early-evening light.

These two scenes, brief as they were, reminded me that it was not my job to hold it all together. So long as I tried to preserve my carefully crafted expectations, unexpected inner terrors and rabbits were sure to pull it all apart. What is being asked of me now? I asked myself. And immediately, a voice seemed to respond. Have faith: Wherever you are is where you belong. Involuntarily, I took a long, deep breath. As soon as I did so, the energy that had concentrated heavily in my head shifted back to my chest, the trembling eased, the sounds filled out. Soon my body quieted, and the rapid beating of my heart slowed down. I will do my work, I said to myself, and let someone else do the rest.

Free now to be guided by their own inclination, my hands sunk deep into a progression of low, resonant chords in the bottom of the piano. Slowly, they built into an energetic crescendo that almost shook the piano and filled the hall. Gradually, this movement evolved into something else, and then into something else again. There was a truthfulness in my playing now that I hadn't felt comfortable to expose before. Why is this truthfulness so important, I wondered. Can't I just sit down and play? But there is more to it than that. I know that when I step onto this stage, just focusing on technique and what I have played before is not enough. It is being truthful to the moment that counts. That is all a performer can depend on. Even though it offers no guarantees, it is all that I have to give. Once that shift occurred, what had at first seemed like hours now felt like minutes, and all too soon it was over.

After the concert, there was a stillness in the hall. The memory of the passing of the glass of water in the prison chapel a year or so before had been a reminder that there was no need to turn my music into a performance, because for me, the sharing of the music has always stood for something else. It was to trust that whatever feelings were living in me in that moment were also in the room. There was nothing to hide. The power of this truth brought tears to my eyes. I have heard this said by others, but this was no substitute for that intimate, timeless moment when I had experienced this truth for myself. I was saddened to remember how often I had taken great pains to manage appearances so as to conceal the truth. It was that concern for appearances that I had brought with me onto the stage that evening. But it was clear that it would fail me, for the desire to look good did not have sufficient inspiration or energy behind it to sustain me through the night. All of this had been given to me in the passing of a glass of water. It was an act of caring that had been done for its own sake one afternoon—it was also a symbolic act of kindness and consideration that had been the source of my salvation the night of my performance. These acts are rarely seen by a crowd. They often occur behind the glare of the lights. Perhaps our finest achievements come this way. Our ambitions may influence us to overshoot or undershoot, but the heart finds its own level, a reminder that life's great moments can often be found in the small. I also felt full in the knowledge that as I opened myself to the audience, they had also opened themselves to me. The sounds that now lingered in the hall belonged to us all. "When have you ever been made less by dying?" Rumi asks.

> From earth you became plant,
> from plant you became an animal,
> Afterwards you became a human being,
> Endowed with knowledge, intellect and faith . . .
> When have you ever been made less by dying,
> When you pass from human form,
> No doubt you will become an angel and soar through the heavens . . .

I did die when I stepped out onto the stage that night. Some-times, it is only through "dying" into our terror that we create a space inside for the more essential part of ourselves to do its work. This essential part is open space, expansive and boundless; it is not restricted to the limiting beliefs that so often cloud our mind. Too often we end up pushing against the very forces that are the true source of our inspiration and strength. We struggle as if life were a dress rehearsal, rather than rest in the moment-to-moment pleasure of feeling what we feel and simply being ourselves. When I and the audience joined together that night, we met in a field of silence that was much more vast than any of our daily preoccupa-tions or concerns. Perhaps if our personalities knew that it is this peacefulness that awaits us, they would release their grip upon us and let this greater love be our true guide. This love finds it source in the underlying essence of who we are. It assures us, as Rumi once said, that while there may be many lamps, there is only one light. No matter how much the surface forms of our life may change, the undying spirit that informs it all remains the same.

Joining the Dance of Creation

I am convinced that if there is magic on the earth it is to be found in or near water. And the waters that most compelled me are among the islands of Georgian Bay. The bay is a mystical place. Along its rugged eastern shore are scattered thousands of small islands, each a host to one or more bent pines, their trunks twisted and gnarled by the battering west winds. Their boughs sometimes offer protection to the wildflowers growing in the soil that collects in the crevices below. These cracks, sculpted by the glaciers that scoured this shore many millennia before, are the only feature that breaks the smooth contours of these rugged, wild granite islands.

We each have a place that offers inspiration and renewal. The quiet water of a secluded lake, the sunny glade deep in the forest, or an alpine meadow bathed in cool, fresh mountain air. It's a place, real or imagined, where the water runs deeper and the sun

shines brighter. For me, what I return to most often are the pines and the rocks and the waters of Georgian Bay.

With broad strokes, I guide my canoe through the narrow protected channels among the islands. Then I see a break in the rock and paddle out into the choppy, open waters. The wind blows full against my face. The canoe bounces hard against the waves. Slowly, I let my eyes rest on the far shore. What I love most about being on these waters is the movement and the space. It is a reminder of something old, like an ancient time when there was only the water, the sky, the wind, the pines, and the rock.

In the beginning was the silence, and from the silence appeared the word. The word was sound and the sound was love. The first language spoken on the earth was song. It is a living tone, a vibration, a reminder that through our song we loved the world into existence. Behind our fears and concerns we are still creators; that song lives in us still. Our ancestors were intimately familiar with this song; it resonated in their language and gave meaning to their life. But for most of us, it is now very faint. Yet it can still be heard in wild places like those close to moving water or deep in the old forests that hug the shore, and in the silent pulse that beats in our hearts. It becomes known to us in those quiet moments when we feel that deep but familiar longing that speaks of what we truly want. It can also be heard in the words of others, especially when the words are formed with care, expressing the truth of the moment and therefore deeply felt. The contours of the formations of the natural world appear to conform to the vibrational forms of sound. As we learn to orient our lives so that they are in harmony with this tone, the manner in which we express ourselves, no matter how it is done, becomes our song. Living an imaginative life connects us with this music and invites it to be a part of our world. Then it is no longer confined to remote places; it becomes the center point of our life.

Here on these waters, I am reminded that the world is my teacher. I feel the presence of all those who have preceded me. I am reminded of what the world was like for the millions of years that ancient people trod lightly across its surfaces, careful to take only what was most needed, because they knew that, out of their respect for this earth, they must also be willing to give it back. I listen for music that is obedient to this silence, tones that honor and celebrate its quiet dignity and majesty. I do so without wishing to impose or intrude myself upon it, knowing that this is my gift and, perhaps even more, an offering of myself as I grow downward and feel my roots taking hold in the rock and sinking deep into the earth.

It is as natural for us to give as it is for the trees to bloom and the animals to dance. It is the means by which we are able to give form to the life that rises up from within us, to give our own voice to the world. The wilderness connects us with this voice; it reminds us from where it has come. When I live in partnership with this authority, I feel at one with the rocks, and the water, and the pines. I am reminded that I am working with something greater than my own self-conscious intentions. I am serving another part of myself, one that is in intimate contact with the dance of creation that surrounds me, one that has always considered this home. The part of myself that has always wanted to feel strong and self-sufficient feels helpless here, knowing that I cannot force this indifferent world do to my bidding any more than I can force these rocks or trees to conform to my plans.

"Excel when you must," an old song from west Africa says. "But do not excel the world." I am humbled by the proportions of everything around me, the sense that the world is greater than anything I can do to it. But I can learn to be obedient to its basic impulse and through my creations fulfill my part of a larger plan. I can let the uniqueness of my voice join with the rest. I can be a part of the emerging chorus, whose collective voice may reawaken the sense of longing and wonder that slumbers still and, in so doing, dissolve some of the layers of doubt and fear that separate us from the fertile ground from which all life and creation come.

"Trees do not force their sap," Rilke reminds us. "Nor does the flower push its bloom." John Keats says our work should come "as naturally as the leaves to a tree, [or] it had better not come at all." There is labor here, but much of the labor is in learning how to allow room for the workings of this greater spirit. What is it that wants to make itself known through us without force or command? Is there something that comes as naturally to us as the leaves to a tree or to a flower its bloom?

To hear creation speak, it helps to return to these wild places, to observe how the spirit I bring to my work is in harmony with the same spirit that moves the birds and the trees, to be reminded that creation is, at its core, engaged for the pure and simple joy of it and not always with the intention of achieving any particular goal.

"All great things are done for their own sake," Robert Frost once said. When we are drawn to step close and penetrate the mystery of whatever it is that represents greatness in our own lives, we discover that it lives in a dimension separate from ours. As soon as we try to get anything from it, or subject it to close examination, it dissolves. Its fullness lies in its infinite potential, the possibility that it can be this and can also be that. Greatness may be found most often in the smallest of acts. Even a simple smile holds a concentration and focus to it, a gentle intensity that is sometimes diluted as soon as it changes into a laugh.

How do we hold to this fine edge in our work without pressing forward or holding back? It is this balance I search for in the music; and as I seek to find it, it becomes clear that it is not only the music I am forming here, but myself. It is inventing me just as I am inventing it. New ideas appear unexpectedly; connections develop between seemingly unrelated or divergent ideas. The feel or sound of a note changes in an instant. When I find the balance, that delicate point between doing too much or too little, of not knowing whether I am moving it or it is moving me, the inherent abundance and generosity of the invisible realms are revealed. It is then that I know we have only to ask, and it will just give and give.

The wind has become stronger now. I turn the canoe toward shore. As I do, a large monarch butterfly glides past me. Then it perches for a moment on the gunnel. Its brilliant orange and black coloring offers a striking contrast to the opaque blue waters beneath me. Then it's off again, swooping up and down as it's carried even farther from shore. I admire its lightness, like a membrane—transparent, delicate, and refined.

Why? I ask. Why struggle out here in this strong wind when it could be comfortably settled among the protected bushes close to shore? Perhaps it is simply to have a taste of freedom, to savor the pleasure of not knowing where it has come from, where it is going, or why. How much is lost when we insist that we must live reasonable lives. "Mysteries are not to be solved," William Blake once said. "The eye goes blind when it only wants to see *why*." Whereas the mind is here to learn what must be done, he reminds us that "the soul is here for its own joy."

When I can let go, even for a moment, of my logical mind's incessant need for reason and explanation, I am given a gift of truly magnificent proportions. I am offered a glimpse of the beauty of the world. And I am reminded of one of the reasons for which I came. It is to give this world—including the innocence and wonder of a child's laughter, the play of light on a sun-drenched lake, the echo of rolling thunder rumbling across the distant hills, and the sadness of the wind as it howls through the tall pines— a musical voice. It is a voice that has been offered for my use while I am here. But when I try to possess it and make it solely mine, it reminds me that its true home lies in another world, one that I can never fully understand. If the world were only facts and logic, what would be the point of it? I love the mystery and find faith in knowing that there is no one right way. If the wind and the waves could talk, I believe that they would agree that our purpose here is not to try to control this world but to set it free, to let each thing evolve freely, to experience itself fully and find its own way. I feel no compulsion to unravel or penetrate these mysteries. Instead, I am reassured when they appear and I hope that they are here to stay.

This is what I love about being at the piano: the exhilaration of feeling music flow through my fingers that is different from what I had planned for that day, the excitement of listening to the emergence of a new idea being born, the sense of not knowing what I have created or what it might mean until it is done, even the regret of seeing many long hours of work lost in what appears to be a dead end. When I can hold all of this without grasping any of it too tightly, I am able to "kiss the joy as it flies."

"Do not be content with the stories of others," Rumi says to us, instead, "unfold your own myth." Each of us is designed to create; our birthright is to live imaginative and original lives. When we are willing to reclaim our story for ourselves, we are fulfilling our destiny. Each day will be an opportunity to "live in eternity's sunrise."

I am back in the bay again. The water is calm here. I hear the wind whistling through the pines on the island nearby. I notice the wildflowers dancing in the breeze, and I am reminded of Faust, to whom the spirits once said, "We were always here, but you did not see us."

The sun is high now; it warms me. I notice how the flowers open their petals to meet the midday light. They do so not from some need for attention or to perform or entertain. It is a spontaneous and unconditionally open-hearted act of generosity. I join with them now in what was the first song of humanity, the joyful cry, "I am!"

Printed in the United States
By Bookmasters